Be Your Best

BY KATHY PEEL

Published by Ballantine Books

THE FAMILY MANAGER'S
GUIDE FOR WORKING MOMS

THE FAMILY MANAGER'S
EVERYDAY SURVIVAL GUIDE

BE YOUR BEST:
The Family Manager's Guide
to Personal Success

BE YOUR BEST

The Family Manager's Guide to Personal Success

KATHY PEEL

◆

BALLANTINE BOOKS ■ NEW YORK

A Ballantine Book
Published by The Ballantine Publishing Group
Copyright © 2000 by Family Manager, Inc.

www.randomhouse.com/BB/

Library of Congress Cataloging-in-Publication Data
Peel, Kathy, 1951–
Be your best : the family manager's guide to personal success / Kathy Peel.
p.   cm.
ISBN 0-345-41984-7 (alk. paper)
1. Women—Time management—United States.   2. Family—Time management—United States.   3. Women—Conduct of life—United States.
4. Home economics—United States.   I. Title.
HQ1221.P37   2000
640'.43'082—dc21   97-52298
CIP

Cover design by Cathy Colbert
Cover photo by Mathew Barnes
Text design by Ann Gold

Manufactured in the United States of America

First Edition: April 2000

10 9 8 7 6 5 4 3 2 1

ACKNOWLEDGMENTS

I am blessed with many people who believe in and support me on a day-to-day, do-it-now-request basis.

Many thanks . . .

To Jodi Thomas, my brilliant, good-humored, overqualified executive assistant and computer maven, for her ability to read my mind.

To Jan Johnson and Holly Halverson, miracle-working editors.

To my friends in the Random House/Ballantine family and at the William Morris Agency, for believing in the big picture.

Most of all, thanks to Bill, John, Joel, and James, my husband and three boys, who spur me on to be my best.

THE FAMILY MANAGER'S CREED

I oversee an organization—
Where hundreds of decisions are made daily,
Where property and resources are managed,
Where health and nutritional needs are determined,
Where finances and futures are discussed and debated,
Where projects are planned and events are arranged,
Where transportation and scheduling are critical,
Where team-building is a priority,
Where careers begin and end.
I oversee an organization—
I am a Family Manager.

CONTENTS

Be Your Best

A New Beginning for You

"Today is when everything that's going to happen from now on begins."   —Harvey Firestone, Jr.

The fact that you've picked up this book tells me that we are probably a lot alike. You're a busy woman—a family manager with myriad responsibilities: budgets, schedules, food, housecleaning and maintenance, birthday parties, vacations, relationships with family and friends, to name a few.

You may also have another full- or part-time job in the marketplace or in the community as a volunteer. Maybe on top of that you've gone back to school. No matter how many jobs you're juggling at a given moment, the real challenge in your life and mine is not so much managing our time, our family, our money, or our countless other responsibilities, but managing ourselves. Everything else depends on this.

This book is about beginning today to use every moment we can find—in nooks and crannies of our lives we never thought of—to take care of ourselves in mind, body, and spirit. It's about expanding our horizons, trying new ways of doing things, taking control of our lives, and moving toward our personal best.

The problem is we can't stop long enough to figure out how to take control of our lives and make some needed changes. We've

> "You had better live your best and act your best and think your best today; for today is the sure preparation for tomorrow and all the other tomorrows that follow."
>
> —Harriet Martineau

already got information overload. It's a dilemma in the life of every busy woman I know. We all have countless things to remember every hour of every day. Knowing personally what this feels like, I don't want this book to overwhelm you with more information. But I'm asking you to trust me, because I know from experience that if you apply the strategies in this book, you will begin to create a better life for you and your family.

You'll find a lot of ideas you can implement immediately that will make noticeable changes in your life right away. There are also strategies that will help you make some really big changes, like discarding destructive habits and embracing new life-enhancing habits, and these will take some time. I don't know what will happen to you as a result of reading this book, but there are many possibilities. You may see how to set aside an hour each day for exercise and self-care, which will give you the energy and endurance you need to be a better wife, mother, professional, and friend. You may decide to take a risk and act on a dream that's been incubating in your mind. You may recognize that you've settled for mediocrity in some areas of your life and begin to live on a higher plane. You may make some small changes that cause you to feel happier, less restless, and more content.

At the end of each chapter you'll find a short section called "The Bottom Line." Here you'll find quick-read points to ponder that will help you be more conscious of taking control of your life and moving toward personal success. You can copy the ones you don't want to forget and post them where you'll see them—on the wall behind your baby's changing table, on the front

of the refrigerator, or on the
dashboard of your car. Or
keep this book in an accessible place, and with a book-
mark or Post-it mark the ideas

> "Do not think of today's
> failures, but of the success that
> may come tomorrow."
> —Helen Keller

that speak to you. Doing this just might be that first small step you
need to take to move toward the best version of yourself.

I hope that this book inspires you to do some serious thinking
about your life—what you want to do, who you want to be, and
where you want to go. As you embark upon this personal journey,
cut yourself some slack on the days when you fall back into old
habit patterns. Failing is not when we fall down; it's when we stay
down. Know that setbacks are normal and serve as stepping-stones
to a better path—a path that leads to a life of personal success. Let
each day herald a new beginning, as Anne of Green Gables said,
"fresh, with no mistakes in it."

ONE

The Best Version
of You

"We must never try to escape the obligation of living at
our best."   —Janet Erskine Stuart

Okay, I know some of you are wondering what planet Janet Erskine Stuart is from. You're thinking, *Living at my best...
ha! How can I, a woman who worships at Our Lady of Perpetual Motion, whose calendar is booked into eternity, find time to even think about my best—let alone find time to work on being it?*

Believe me, I hear you. I understand your skepticism. But before you give up on finding time to improve your life and throw this book into your recycling bin, let's take a look at some of the stereotypes you may have in your head when you think about women who have taken control of their lives and are growing into who they want to be.

Which Describes You Best?

With pen in hand and tongue in cheek, read the following descriptions of different types of women. Which one(s) are you? Check all that apply.

_____ **Type 1:** Wears a perfect size 6; sports an up-to-date hairstyle that always looks good; has a personal trainer, a nanny, a cook, a housekeeper, and plenty of money to pay for them.

____ **Type 2:** Born with a rare self-discipline gene the rest (most) of us are missing.

____ **Type 3:** A cousin of the one with the self-discipline gene, a natural-born charismatic extrovert to whom everything in life comes easily.

____ **Type 4:** A woman with a clock and a calendar instead of a life and with absolutely no clue what the flowers smell like.

____ **Type 5:** A woman who discovered a genie in a bottle during her daily run on the beach. She got her wish for a twenty-five-hour day, so now she has time to spare.

____ **Type 6:** A gifted manager with an MBA from a top-notch university who capably manages every single aspect of her personal, family, and professional life—including her children and umpteen employees—without once taking a deep breath. (Did I mention her ability to leap tall buildings in a single bound?)

____ **Type 7:** None of the above.

If you checked only one box, the last, I'd say you're like most of the women I encounter in the course of my days—including the one woman I meet in the mirror every morning.

If you hold unrealistic ideas about what it means to be personally successful, more than likely you learned what you believe from the media. Billions of advertising dollars are spent each year to help you and me define personal success, and many times, to our own detriment, we buy into these messages.

Advertisements show us people who are happily married and set for life because they use the right credit card; commercials tell us that women can have it all—the perfect home, husband, job, and life— if they eat the right kind of cereal; retailers flood our mailboxes with catalogs that portray impossible ideals. Most

> "Don't take anyone else's definition of success as your own." —Jacqueline Briskin

readers don't realize that the models in these photographs have had lithographic liposuction—computers have whittled away their buttocks and thighs.

Marketing experts report that consumers pay over $4 billion a year on impulse purchases that appeal to the top three desires by which they

> "So many of us define ourselves by what we have, what we wear, what kind of house we live in and what kind of car we drive. . . . If you think of yourself as the woman in the Cartier watch and the Hermès scarf, a house fire will destroy not only your possessions but yourself." —Linda Henley

measure personal success and satisfaction: money, sex, and beauty. Buying opportunities abound for products that promise instant answers and overnight change. "You can't be too rich or too thin too soon" is the mantra of the day.

What Does Personal Success Look Like to You?

We've all been inspired by stories about men and women who had a dream: they wanted to start their own business, climb Mount Everest, or raise millions of dollars for a good cause. For example, as a young girl, Jane Addams saw poor children and dreamed of helping them. She founded Hull House in Chicago, a home for those lacking one. She continued her work on behalf of people everywhere and in 1931 won the Nobel Peace Prize. Before one package was ever delivered by Federal Express, Fred Smith, a modern entrepreneur, dreamed of a fast, efficient system of getting packages from one place to another overnight. These endeavors had their roots in dreams.

Yes, stories such as these are inspirational, but they can also be overwhelming. What if I don't want to win the Nobel Peace Prize or start my own business? What if all I want to do is get my teaching certificate or take care of my family or lose thirty pounds or clean out the garage?

> "Nothing happens unless first a dream." —Carl Sandburg

Sometimes even the smallest dreams can have a profound impact. You don't have to find a cure for cancer or a way to end poverty worldwide to make a significant difference in the quality of your life, your family, and the world around you. The power and influence of one person who decides to take control of his or her life and strive for personal success is far-reaching.

Sadly, though, not everyone feels the freedom to dream about personal success. I meet women regularly who believe that success, whether personal or professional, is experienced only by great people—and they don't feel a part of that elite group. Other women I meet say they stopped dreaming at a young age when they were reprimanded about daydreaming in elementary school. Still others are afraid to dream because they tried to change their lives once and faced setbacks and rejections. They felt as though they'd failed and now they are determined never to try again.

As you think about getting control of your life, it is important to consider what personal success looks like to you. The question is simple but revolutionary because it suggests that the answer comes from inside you rather than what . . . .

your family expects you to be.

your spouse wants you to be.

your boss pressures you to be.

your employees need you to be.

your friends tell you to be.

society wants you to be.

> "If you don't have a plan for yourself, you'll be part of someone else's."
> —American proverb

Dreaming Exercise

Imagine that there are no restrictions or obstacles in your life. You can do what you want to do and be who you want to be. Make a list of ten things you would do if this were true.

1. _____

2. _____

3. _____

4. _____

5. _____

6. _____

7. _____

8. _____

9. _____

10. _____

When I first tackled this exercise twelve years ago it was difficult for me to get past the "no restrictions or obstacles" part. I wanted to edit each dream with "but" or "if only" or "there's no way." I finally allowed myself to write down my first dream: to write books and share with other women what I had learned about raising kids and running a home. I had to disregard the "restrictions" that I didn't have a degree in journalism and didn't know the first thing about getting published. Now, fifteen books later, I'm glad I gave myself the freedom to write down my dream. That was the first step in making it come true.

Boiled Frog:
The Consequences of Standing Still

I am not the least bit fond of frogs, but one classic biology experiment with a frog has always fascinated me. The experiment begins with a frog in a pot of cold water. The pot is set over a stove burner, which is turned on. As the water gradually heats up, although the frog has the ability to jump out, it chooses to remain in the pot. Result: It slowly boils to death. The frog does not notice the slight increases in temperature until it is too late to take action.

Many women I meet remind me of the frog. They say their lives are uncomfortable, maybe even out of control. But they don't move; they choose to survive rather than thrive. They tolerate discomfort and chaos in their lives because it's easier to blame external circumstances than to accept the responsibility to change. They don't realize how this kind of attitude is affecting them until the results are harmful, to themselves and those around them.

"I'll make time to exercise when the kids are older." Boiled frog.

"I'll take a step toward my dreams when my schedule slows down." Boiled frog.

"I'll look for a job where I can better use my skills and talents when we get the mortgage paid off." Boiled frog.

"I'll deal with the unresolved conflict with my husband when things settle down at work." Boiled frog.

"I'll seek professional help for my destructive habit pattern when I have more money." Boiled frog.

Our society as a whole has adopted a victim mentality about life. We blame

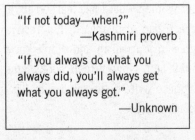

"If not today—when?"
—Kashmiri proverb

"If you always do what you always did, you'll always get what you always got."
—Unknown

our age, health, financial circumstances, peers, spouse, or
handicaps, when what we're
really saying is "Poor me." All
of us face circumstances that

> "Think of what you can do with
> what there is."
> —Ernest Hemingway

hinder change in our lives. Our attitude deteriorates. Our vision
blurs. Our courage wanes. We feel overwhelmed and focus on our
liabilities, some of which are real but are greatly exaggerated, and
some of which are imagined. What we must do instead is *choose*
(the operative word here, because we do have a choice) to focus
on our assets—what we do have and what we can do.

Taking Control of Your Life

I grew up in Memphis not far from where Elvis lived before he
built Graceland. As a young girl, I often asked my mother to let me
sit out on the curb in front of his house to watch for him. I saw
him quite a few times.

Many people have tried to understand what happened to this
man of incredible fame and fortune. Why did his life end so tragi-
cally? I believe it's because he lost control. He lost control of
his appetite, his emotions, his relationships, his business af-
fairs, and his career. Friends of mine who knew Elvis say he sur-
rounded himself with people who always gave him what he
wanted. No one could control him, and he was unable to control
himself.

BIT BY BIT

Maybe you're thinking, *Well, I complain about my life being out
of control, but it's not that bad!* Hopefully it's not. But total lack
of control doesn't just happen overnight. When we choose not
to take control of our lives, we fall prey to destructive habits,

> "We cannot do everything at once, but we can do something at once." —Calvin Coolidge

poor decisions, and a less-than-satisfying life. When we put off making changes, we allow little problems to grow into big ones. When we settle for mediocrity instead of pursuing what we know is best, we surrender our chances for personal success.

Women who have taken control of their lives and who manage their time and their physical, spiritual, mental, and emotional health and growth well were not born that way. The discipline needed to take control of your life and move toward personal success can be developed. The skills can be learned. The drive is within all of us. A marathon runner is no different from you or me in terms of the ability to dream and to work toward her dream. She had to start someplace. She just worked toward her goal a little each day. Her small achievements—a one-mile walk, a one-mile run, a five-mile run—eventually added up to a big one: a twenty-six-plus-mile run. Bit by bit is the only way to achieve personal success of any kind.

Every time I begin a new book I relearn the bit-by-bit approach to getting things done. First, I write and pitch the proposal. I know what I want the book to be about. I can even see it in my mind. I sign the contract. And then I go home and start to stew. I'm thinking *book*, and that's a big word. A book has several hundred pages in it. I have to write them all. How am I ever going to do it? I dither and make false starts. Then when I've pretty much frustrated myself and my editor, I sit down with a hodgepodge of notes and random sentences and begin to figure out, bit by bit, what goes in the first chapter, what in the second chapter, and so on.

A book gets written word by word. A life gets lived day by day, hour by hour. If I don't pay attention to the individual words and thoughts, I never finish the book. If I don't take advantage of the small opportunities on a daily basis—five minutes for silent contemplation of the blessings in my life, ten minutes for a brisk walk between appointments, an hour a week to take a class I'm interested

> "Life isn't a matter of milestones, but of moments."
> —Rose Fitzgerald Kennedy

in—I never experience how they add up to big changes.

Losing thirty pounds might start with increasing my level of activity five minutes a day or drinking more water every day. If I give myself credit for the baby steps I take today, I'm more likely to take bigger steps tomorrow. None of us expects a one-year-old who's just learning to walk to run across a playground. Yet we seem to have different expectations for ourselves.

A friend of mine, a banker turned full-time family manager, is a case in point. She has three children under the age of six and a household out of control in every way. For years she had dreamed of starting a family, quitting her job at the bank, and creating a smooth-running, low-stress home where family members could develop to their full potential. Well, the first two parts of her dream came to pass, but when it came to the part about her home, it wasn't happening. The resulting stress caused her to invite me over one day for coffee and consultation.

When I entered her home, I understood anew the way clutter can take over your life. Even though my friend's family had moved into the house more than a year earlier, she still hadn't unpacked everything. Toys, boxes, and piles of papers were everywhere. She had never found the necessary blocks of time, she explained, to finish moving in. She was close to despair. "If I can run a trust department of a bank, why can't I run my home? I feel like such a failure."

Her husband's frustration added to her guilt. When he came home at nine o'clock, having worked a fourteen-hour day at his law office, he reacted to the chaos.

A vicious cycle was in operation: there was so much to do that my friend couldn't get motivated to do anything. So the piles and tension remained.

My friend hoped I would bring over a magic wand, and presto-chango, no more mess. She just knew that Kathy Peel, the Family Manager, would change her life, in the same way Samantha on *Bewitched* used to wiggle her nose and instantly fix everything. Unfortunately, I had to tell her that I knew of no quick way to get rich, thin, or organized. Each of these processes happens bit by bit.

So I put her on an action plan, doing a little bit at a time, with our goal being a clutter-free, decorated, organized home in five months. Maybe she has only fifteen minutes a day when a child isn't clamoring for her attention, but that's fifteen minutes of unpacking, sorting, and putting away, and those piles *will* diminish over time. (We're starting with the family room first so her husband will soon have at least one restful-looking room to sit in when he gets home.) "In process," I emphasized to my friend, is okay—which is a good thing, because that's the way most of life is!

Getting Unstuck

All of us get in a stuck-state every once in a while. We feel so overwhelmed, so buried under the pile of life that we can't see how to make even small changes. We don't see that we have any choices and feel as though our life is totally out of our control.

> "No great thing is created suddenly."   —Epictetus
>
> "I'm not there yet, but I'm closer than I was yesterday."   —Unknown

Sure, some things *are* totally outside of our control—our race, sex, age, family of origin, physical attributes, and other people's choices. But there are countless other things in our lives that are within our control—for example, our feelings, thoughts, values, education, wellness, attitudes, training, and problem-solving skills.

There have been many times in my life when I've felt stuck without options to do something I really wanted to do, but one time in particular comes to mind. When our sons were ages twelve, eight, and one, I decided if I didn't do something to stimulate my own personal growth, my mind might turn to mush. I longed to do something creative besides fingerpaint and build Lego cities. I dreamed of once again taking piano lessons and expressing myself on the keyboard, something I hadn't done since my teenage years. But I felt stuck. We couldn't afford for me to take piano lessons since we were already over budget with the children's education and extracurricular activity costs. And even if we'd had the money to pay for lessons, we didn't have a piano at home for me to practice on.

Well, I had learned early in life to see problems from different angles: come up with fresh solutions, perspectives, and approaches rather than settling for what I'm told is the limit. When I was eight years old I wanted very badly to win an Easter egg hunt. I realized I couldn't win because my basket was smaller than everyone else's, so I put my basket down and grabbed the hem of my dress to form a big pocket in which to collect eggs. At the end of the contest my dress was weighted down with eggs. I won! (The next year the judges of the contest made a new rule that you had to collect the eggs in a basket.)

I applied this creative problem-solving method to my piano-lesson dilemma and began to noodle on the situation. I decided to call the local college to find out if they had a music department, and if so, if they had any scholarships

> "Nothing will ever be attempted if all possible obstacles must be first overcome." —Samuel Johnson

available. Yes, they did, on both counts. Then I had to come up with a piano. At this time, our two older boys were both involved in sports and other activities at our church three days a week. Usually I just took a book to read while waiting for them on those days. I asked the church for permission to practice on one of their pianos instead. They were happy for me to do this. Problem solved. Later that year we were able to buy a used piano.

Use your imagination. If you find yourself at a roadblock, come up with new routes.

Can't afford to join a gym? Walk. Buy or rent a workout video.

Can't afford a new wardrobe? Check out used-clothing stores.

Can't take a class right now? Research the topic at the library and read up on it on your own.

Can't invest time in a spiritual retreat? Choose an inspirational book to read with a friend. Talk about it together.

Can't fit a thirty-minute aerobic session into today's schedule? Park some distance from your office and walk briskly. Mow the lawn with a push mower. Take the kids to a playground and play *with* them.

And remember to enlist support. If you're having trouble coming up with creative alternatives to problems, ask someone you know to help you see things in a different light. They'll be able to give you a different perspective.

Credit Where Credit Is Due

All of us need to give ourselves credit for thinking creatively and taking whatever steps we can toward making changes in our lives and moving in the direction of our dreams. Applause, please, for:

> "In the middle of difficulty lies opportunity."
> —Albert Einstein

- The weary thirty-year-old divorced mother of two who holds down two jobs but who still arranges for her sister-in-law to take care of her kids on a Saturday afternoon so she can attend a women's health conference.
- The forty-seven-year-old with a dream of starting a home-based catering business who creates a logo and has business cards printed up.
- The fifty-year-old bank teller who writes away for her high school transcript as the first step toward finishing her college degree, one night class at a time.
- The forty-year-old finally blessed with a baby after years of trying who gives herself permission to take a nap when the baby does.
- The exercise-phobe who decides to walk for just ten minutes a day. And does it, four days out of seven.
- The mother longing for adult company who posts a notice in her supermarket looking for other moms with young kids to form a play group.
- The woman who wants to lose weight who reaches for carrot sticks instead of potato chips.
- Countless women everywhere who put their teakettles on and spend fifteen minutes with their feet up this afternoon.

Who knows where these steps will lead? The bank teller may get her degree about the time she reaches retirement age. The exercise-phobe may end up running a marathon. Or these two may just enjoy the process of taking classes and walking. At any rate, they have taken their needs seriously and acted on those needs, with far-reaching effects.

Give Yourself Credit

Think bit by bit. Over the next few days, write down the small steps you take that you deserve credit for. Maybe you'll choose to drink water instead of a sugary soda, send in your registration for a continuing-education seminar, set your alarm fifteen minutes earlier. Whatever smart choices you make, use this space to jot them down. Come back to them when you need to remind yourself that you are making progress.

1. _____

2. _____

3. _____

4. _____

5. _____

6. _____

A question to ask myself every day: What can I do today, this hour, this minute to progress toward taking control of my life?

An answer: It doesn't have to be bigger than a bread box. It's the little things that add up.

Important Questions You Need to Answer

What is the worst thing that could happen if I took a step toward getting control of my life?

_____

_____

What is the best thing that could happen if I took a step toward getting control of my life?

_____

_____

What will happen if I don't make some changes in my life?

_____

_____

The Bottom Line

- Personal success means exactly that: moving toward _your_ dreams and plans, not someone else's ideas for you.
- If you've been living in a rut for a number of years, surviving but not thriving, realize that a rut can be quite powerful. Many times it's easier to stay in the rut, even if it's unpleasant or uncomfortable. Remind yourself regularly that you don't want to be a boiled frog.
- Identifying areas ripe for change in your life is not about whining or finding fault with yourself or others. It's also not about listing excuses for why you can't initiate change: "I'll do it as soon as someone else does something else." "I don't have this tool or that money or that kind of support." "I can't because this or that will make it harder."

- By consciously making choices that positively influence your circumstances—bit by bit—you exert more control over your life. Every choice you make, from the smallest, like taking the stairs instead of the elevator, to the biggest, like changing jobs so you can have more flextime, moves you closer or farther away from the person you want to become and the life you want to have.

- The woman who decides to take control of her life exhibits no particular style except her own. She doesn't necessarily have a lot of money to hire experts—a personal trainer, a private language tutor, a housekeeper, or a therapist. On the other hand, she may well rely on the advice and services of experts when she needs them, juggling her financial resources to get the maximum benefit from them. She may or may not have another career outside her home. The one sure thing is that she—like me, like you, like all of us—is working from where she is today, doing what she can do with the time and resources she's got.

- Whether you're able to make great strides or small ones toward becoming the woman you want to be, all strides are worth making. Every stride is a single step. As Lao-tzu says, "a journey of one thousand miles begins with a single step."

TWO

Putting a Value on You
(Think High)

"Too many people overvalue what they are not and undervalue
what they are."   —Malcolm Forbes

The bathroom was growing mold. The back of my closet was
full of clothes I hadn't worn since platform shoes were in the
first time, and who knows what was in that stack of boxes in
the garage that wobbled every time I slammed the car door?

I was terminally busy, running around trying to meet the needs
of three growing boys and a husband, balancing a home-based
business and a zillion volunteer commitments. Taking care of myself was certainly not as important as taking care of everyone and
everything else on my to-do list. And even if it were, when would I
fit it in?

So I continued to ignore all the warning signs and scrambled
to meet each day's demands with no thought of stopping. Then
I reached a point where I had to make some changes or crash
and burn.

You probably know the feeling; it's similar to trying to stretch a
paycheck farther and farther, juggling debits every day. Instead,
I learned, we would do better to think of ourselves as checking
accounts—with limits. And if your checking account is like mine,
you need a buffer, at the bank and in life. Hardly a day goes by that

> "My mind is overtaxed. Brave and courageous as I am, I feel the creeping on of that inevitable thing, a breakdown, if I cannot get some immediate relief. I need somebody to come and get me."
> —Mary McLeod Bethune

we don't experience some type of unexpected "withdrawal" that drains us physically or emotionally. Too many withdrawals and not enough deposits always ends in disaster.

Are You Headed for Burnout?

Answer the following questions to find out just how close you are to burnout. How often do you have any of the following experiences? On the line place the number that reflects your experience, according to the following scale:

1. NEVER
2. ONCE IN A GREAT WHILE
3. RARELY
4. SOMETIMES
5. OFTEN
6. USUALLY
7. ALWAYS

1. Being tired____
2. Feeling depressed____
3. Having a good day____
4. Being physically exhausted____
5. Being emotionally exhausted____
6. Being happy____
7. Being wiped out____
8. Thinking you can't take it anymore____

9. Being unhappy____
10. Feeling run-down____
11. Feeling trapped____
12. Feeling worthless____
13. Being weary____
14. Being troubled____
15. Feeling resentful____
16. Being weak, susceptible to illness____
17. Feeling hopeless____
18. Feeling rejected____
19. Feeling optimistic____
20. Feeling energetic____
21. Feeling anxious____

FIGURE YOUR SCORE

a. Insert check marks beside these numbers: 1, 2, 4, 5, 7, 8, 9, 10, 11, 12, 13, 14, 15, 16, 17, 18, 21

b. Then make Xs beside these numbers: 3, 6, 19, 20

c. Add the values you wrote next to the numbers with check marks. Write that sum here:____

d. Add the values you wrote next to the numbers with Xs. Write that sum here:____

e. Subtract the sum from d from the number 32. Write that number here:____

f. Add your answers in steps c and e, then divide this number by 21. This is your burnout score. (It will probably be a mixed number.)

- If your score is between 2 and 3, you are doing well. (You probably have your life under control and don't need to read this book.)

- If your score is between 3 and 4, you should examine your

> "Ulcers, migraines, nervous tension, and a dozen other symptoms mark our psychic overload. We are concerned not to live beyond our means financially; why do it emotionally?" —Richard Foster

life, think about what matters most to you, and consider making some changes.

- If your score is higher than 4, you are experiencing burnout. (Keep reading this book and begin applying the principles today.)

- If your score is higher than 5, you need immediate help.

We Care for the Things We Value

Hands down, the most common complaint I hear from my friends, colleagues, and countless women I meet across the nation is "I'm so busy caring for others, I don't have time to care for myself." They say they're tired, frustrated, and close to burnout. They have too much to do and not enough time to do it in; practically the last thing they think about is taking care of themselves. They find little pleasure in life. There's no buffer between them and the everyday pressures that mount and mount and mount.

The buffer we all need comes from *self-care*. When we take time to rejuvenate, it pays off in many ways, including being a better mom, wife, friend, or professional and enjoying life a whole lot more. When we don't, that also pays off in many ways. One woman commented, "When I forget my own needs, I become angry at every demand on my time, from my husband to my children to my home to friends to school and church—even the dog!" To fail to invest in our own

> "Researchers strongly agree on two basic principles: first, that man has limited capacity; and second, that overloading the system leads to serious breakdown of performance."
> —Alvin Toffler

value—to fail to build equity in ourselves—through self-care is to put not only ourselves but our families at risk. After all, if I collapse, I'm no good to anyone.

Top Ten Reasons Women Say They Don't Take Care of Themselves

1. *Circumstances.* We live under the tyranny of the urgent: whatever or whoever is screaming the loudest gets the attention—and something or someone is always making noise. One friend calls this "managing by fire"—she deals with whatever is making the most smoke at any given moment.

2. *Others' expectations.* We're all prone to succumb to the agendas of others. Granted, a six-month-old with a soggy diaper doesn't know he's got expectations and is exerting pressure on us. And his requests are reasonable! But sometimes we allow ourselves to be raw material for someone else's intentions. When is the last time you said yes to a request simply because some domineering person asked it of you?

3. *Natural boundaries.* We simply can't do all there is to do with the limited number of hours and amount of energy we have each day. We must make choices that reflect an understanding of this.

4. *Lack of focus.* If we don't examine our situation once in a while, we're never sure what we want or need to be doing because we haven't stopped long enough to figure it out.

5. *Love of comfort.* We all tend to avoid change, if possible. We want few surprises and a minimum of inconvenience, which change always brings, so we avoid the new in favor of the familiar. Consequently we miss out on the good change often brings.

6. *Not enough time.* Actually we do have the time, it's just what we choose to spend it on.

7. *Fear of failure.* Safety has a friendly face, but it's deceptive.

Sometimes the kindest and best thing we can do for ourselves and those we love is take a risk.

8. *Misunderstanding the process.* We guess that taking control of our life so we can build in time for self-care is something we can initiate one day and master the next. The truth is, like any habit or change in lifestyle, it's not an overnight occurrence.

9. *Lack of connection with the big picture.* When our eyes are fixed on getting through just this hour or this day, there's no way we can begin to plan for next week.

10. *Pride.* Sometimes we are simply unwilling to admit our need for change or help.

We can all probably identify with one or more of those reasons, but I believe there is one all-important underlying reason why we don't take care of ourselves: *We don't see ourselves as valuable and worthy of care.*

Let me ask you a question: If I drove up in your driveway today and handed you the keys to a brand-new minivan, free of charge, would you keep it maintained, washed, and filled with gas? I think you would. If I gave you a thoroughbred horse as a present, would you make sure it was fed, brushed, and exercised? Probably so. Why? We take care of the things we deem valuable. It would be an eye-opening experience for many of us if we took a good hard look at what we really do perceive as valuable.

A friend of mine told me a story recently of a woman who has a Pekinese dog. To say the woman values her dog is an understatement. She cares so much for her dog that she ordered an uphol-stered four-poster dog bed, complete with linens, to put beside her own bed. She feeds her dog the most expensive kind of dog food, and buys special "potty pads" so the dog won't have to re-lieve herself outside; after all, the dog might get her paws dirty. And the dog has more toys (including dolls and stuffed animals) than many children have in a lifetime.

While this story may represent an extreme, it can help us think about what we value and care for. There's no getting

> "You know you're in crisis when you can't tell if the bathroom lightbulb is burned out or the house is burning down."
> —Margaret Welshons

around it: what we don't value we don't take care of. And if we don't take care of ourselves, everything will eventually fall apart. To do so is to put not only ourselves but our families at risk.

If we neglect ourselves long enough, a minor catastrophe can become a major issue. A friend told me the story of a time when she neglected herself nearly to the point of no return. For months she coped with a demanding job at the same time as she was going through a difficult divorce. She thought she was doing fine until five o'clock one morning when she discovered that the hot-water heater had sprung a leak. Hot water was gushing onto her basement floor. She took one look at the floor and went into hysterics. At five-thirty she called her ex-husband and three friends, asking them what to do. Finally she was able to perform the simple task of turning off the spigot that led into the heater. The whole incident took so much out of her already-depleted self that she missed three days of work. Nearly a decade later, she still recalls this episode as a dangerously low point in her life.

Though putting your own needs last may seem the right thing to do, the truth is, when you don't take care of yourself, you're not doing yourself, your spouse, or your children any favors. If you're bored, depressed, and restless, your family can't help

> "Love your neighbor as yourself, we're told. Maybe before I can love my neighbor very effectively, I have to love me—not in the sense of a blind passion but in the sense of looking after, of wishing well, of forgiving when necessary, of being my own friend."
> —Frederick Buechner

> "Friendship with oneself is all-important because without it one cannot be friends with anyone else in the world."
> —Eleanor Roosevelt

but know it. And that takes its toll. After all, what are we teaching our children about life if we're constantly tired? If we grumble every Sunday night about going to a job we hate? If we begrudge every errand and chore around the house? If our basic attitude is "I never get to do anything I want to do"?

Love—or the lack of it—forms the foundation of how we see ourselves. When we love people, we're eager and willing to spend time and energy taking care of them, meeting their needs, and watching them flourish. As mothers we want to make sure our children have healthy images of themselves as loving and lovable people. We must present them with good models, which means we must see ourselves as people worth loving and treat ourselves with as much loving-kindness as we lavish on others.

Care begets care. When you honor your own needs and desires, you naturally honor those of others as well. In a family, when the family manager becomes calmer and more pleasant because she's fulfilling a long-held dream in some way, not only does the family benefit from her improved demeanor but she takes their dreams more seriously as well.

The point is, the way we treat ourselves will inevitably affect the way we treat others. Taking care of yourself is a win/win situation.

Unfortunately, most of us weren't raised or trained to value taking care of ourselves. The kids, the husband, the job, the parents, the in-laws, the boss, the volunteer groups—everyone and everything else come first. On the other hand, I'm not asking you to adopt the attitudes of the Me Generation, to abandon your family to join an ashram or to go into debt for plastic surgery.

I'm talking about taking care of yourself so you can be your own personal best, so you can meet the needs and responsibilities of your life. I'm talking about finding slots of time in which you can make your health and serenity a priority. We show that we love others by taking care of

> "We cannot be a source of strength unless we nurture our own strength."
> —M. Scott Peck

them. Is it such a stretch to see that we show love for ourselves by taking care of ourselves? The wonderful thing is, if we value and take better care of ourselves, we have more to give to those we love.

An Official Value of You

It's official. Something I've wanted to believe for years has been quantified: in today's job market a mother is worth more than $500,000 a year. According to a study by Edelman Financial Services, the job description for a typical multitasking mother includes the following:

- raising children
- cooking meals
- keeping house
- caring for pets
- dispensing medication and nursing
- attending meetings and functions
- managing family finances
- providing transportation
- assisting with homework
- listening to and responding to family problems
- keeping family on schedule
- maintaining family order and harmony

If we take into account seventeen key occupations, a mother's financial worth is approximately $507,200 per year, or almost

$42,300 per month. The seventeen key occupations that mothers typically perform, along with their median yearly salaries, are:

- animal caretaker: $17,500
- executive chef: $40,000
- computer systems analyst: $44,000
- financial manager: $39,000
- food/beverage service worker: $20,000
- general office clerk: $19,000
- registered nurse: $35,000
- management analyst: $41,000
- child care worker: $13,000
- housekeeper: $9,000
- psychologist: $29,000
- bus driver: $32,400
- elementary school principal: $58,600
- dietitian/nutritionist: $41,600
- property manager: $22,600
- social worker: $30,000
- recreation worker: $15,500

"Of course, no one can place a value on the love and affection that mothers give to their families," stated Ric Edelman, chairman of Edelman Financial Services. "But since a mother wears many hats and is on duty twenty-four hours a day, we decided that a typical mother deserves a full-time yearly salary for all seventeen key occupational positions."

Enough said?

> "Any mother could perform the jobs of several air-traffic controllers."   —Lisa Alther

Do You See Yourself as Valuable and Worthy of Care? Fifty-two Questions to Answer and Grade Yourself

1. Do you get sufficient rest?
2. Do you eat nutritious foods?
3. Do you get regular physicals?
4. Do you get the facts on any medications prescribed to you?
5. Do you take vitamin supplements?
6. Do you treat yourself to a manicure and pedicure every now and then?
7. Do you purposefully do things you enjoy to unwind—take bubble baths, put on soothing music?
8. Do you give yourself facials and take care of your skin with good products?
9. Do you stay in touch with your friends?
10. Do you keep your closet and drawers organized so that they are visually and functionally pleasing to you?
11. Do you make it a point to spend time with stimulating, up-beat people?
12. Do you exercise regularly?
13. Do you get up early enough to have some quiet time in the morning to think about your day and your life?
14. Do you read books?
15. Are you learning things you want to know more about?
16. Do you plan your day the night before?
17. Do you limit your phone time with chatty friends who waste your spare time?
18. Do you take care of your hair and have the best style for your face and features?
19. Do you wear a fragrance you enjoy?

20. Do you wear pretty undergarments?

21. Do you try to have good posture?

22. Do you buy clothes and accessories that reflect your personality and profession?

23. Do you allow yourself to pursue new hobbies and interests?

24. Do you travel or visit places that interest you?

25. Do you keep your schedule on a calendar or in a planning notebook?

26. Do you allow yourself to take midweek mini-retreats—such as to a museum or a park?

27. Do you collect ideas and quotes that stimulate your thinking to enhance your life?

28. Do you allow yourself to develop your talent and interests in music?

29. Do you attend services or studies that stimulate your spiritual growth and understanding?

30. Do you give yourself breast examinations once a month?

31. If you sit a lot at a desk, is investing in a good desk chair important to you?

32. Do you buy or cut fresh flowers to enjoy at your home or on your desk at the office?

33. Do you make some quiet time to think about where you are in life—your goals and aspirations?

34. Do you keep a journal of your thoughts and prayers?

35. Do you keep a dream file of brochures and articles about faraway places you'd like to visit someday?

36. Do you make sure your environment has a fragrance you enjoy?

37. Do you check out books on tape from your public library for listening and learning in your car?

38. Do you splurge a little every now and then to do or buy something special for yourself?

39. Do you allow yourself to get a massage every so often?
40. Is your bedroom inviting and serene?
41. Do you get regular eye examinations?
42. Do you keep the book you never get to read in your car or purse?
43. Do you allow yourself to learn a craft—maybe pottery making or flower arranging?
44. Do you volunteer your time and talents in ways that are helpful to others and fulfilling to you?
45. Do you reward yourself with something enjoyable when you've finished a big chore or project?
46. Do you give yourself the freedom to take a "mental health day"—taking one day to do what you want to do all day?
47. Do you allow yourself to join a group you're interested in, such as an amateur sports team, an arts and crafts group, a church choir, or a reading circle?
48. Do you allow yourself to cry when you're sad?
49. Do you forgive yourself when you do something stupid?
50. Do you drink six glasses of water a day?
51. Do you make time in your day for reading something inspirational?
52. Do you smile at yourself in the mirror?

Taking control of your life and growing toward your own personal best is, first of all, about seeing yourself as a very valuable person. Add to that what you do in another career in the marketplace or as a volunteer in the community and you can't help but see that you are an important resource to many people. Living a balanced life is vital.

An Exercise in Balance

Personally overdrawn: Maybe that's how you feel. Maybe you're beginning to see yourself as valuable and want to make some changes, but you don't know where to begin. The first step to a balanced life is to establish priorities. Just as we decide which bills get paid first, we need to decide what things come first in our lives. What's really important to you? Where does taking care of yourself fall on your list?

Perhaps you're thinking, *I'm so busy I can't even take the time to sort out my priorities, much less live by them.* Take it from a woman who learned this lesson the hard way: unless you decide that it's vitally important to take an hour or so and go someplace quiet, where you can think about what's important to you, you face a life of daily overdrafts.

Knowing what our priorities are is the first step toward balancing our lives, but that step isn't enough, because priorities aren't really priorities unless we act on them. When your checking account isn't balanced, you have to check debits and credits to figure out where you've messed up. This is a good way to see where you're out of balance in life as well. You might start by keeping a log for just one day. On the left-hand side of a sheet of paper, under Debits, write down every demand on your time. Be honest. If something you thought was going to take fifteen minutes took two hours, write that down. Don't worry about making a bad decision or a bad estimate. Just be honest.

On the right-hand side of your paper, write down the things you do to take care of yourself and the time it takes to do them. Call these Credits. I'm *not* suggesting that the right side should balance with the left. Taking care of ourselves is only one of our responsibilities. This is simply an accounting to see if we're risking overdraft.

At the end of the day, take a look at your columns. Did you spend any time at all on yourself? Are there things in the Debits column that could have been delegated, done differently, or not done at all? What adjustments could you make on the left that would buy you some time to build up your buffer?

Debits

- My son forgot to take his lunch to school. −20 minutes
- The phone rang as I walked out the door for work. When I turned around, I dropped my sunglasses and they broke. The phone call was a wrong number. −10 minutes
- The credit-card company double-billed us for a purchase we made last month. −10 minutes
- A lightning storm zapped our air conditioner. It's 90 degrees outside and climbing on the inside. I searched the attic for our portable fans. I found two, but they were caked in dust. −30 minutes
- I planned on taking half an hour to finish an article, but it wouldn't come together, and it took me two hours, plus I had to phone my editor and say it would be late. −90 minutes
- The dog ran off and I had to drive around looking for him. −20 minutes

Credits

- A neighbor called to ask if I wanted to join a book club that meets monthly; I said yes. I immediately ordered next month's book online. +15 minutes
- I took a lunch break and saw a show at the museum. +45 minutes
- I went on a leisurely after-dinner walk with my husband. +45 minutes

- I called my old college roommate and chatted. We started planning a girls' getaway weekend. +20 minutes
- I squeezed in a bubble bath before bedtime. +15 minutes
- I did fifty sit-ups before bed. +5 minutes
- I read an article in a favorite magazine. +20 minutes

On this sample day my debits add up to 180 and my credits to 165, which means it turned out to be a reasonably sane day despite the setbacks. If you're having trouble figuring out where your life is out of balance you might want to repeat this exercise for several days running.

The Bottom Line

- It's a simple equation. If you're too tired to take care of yourself, you're probably too tired to take care of anybody or anything else well.
- We all need to build buffers in our lives by making self-care "deposits" to withstand the inevitable, unexpected experiences that drain us physically and/or emotionally. Too many of these types of "withdrawals" and not enough deposits always ends in disaster.
- Even though we pay lip service to the idea of taking care of ourselves, many women tend to put themselves at the bottom of the list. Never forget: you are an important asset to your family and your extended family.
- When we value and care for ourselves, we have more to give to those we love.
- The choices we make every hour of every day create our future.

THREE

Small Risks, Big Rewards for You

"Avoiding danger is no safer in the long run than outright exposure. Life is either a daring adventure or nothing."
—Helen Keller

Admittedly, risk is hard for many of us. It's easier to play it safe, to stay in the comfort zone or tolerate the status quo instead of striving for our personal best. It's easier to deny or ignore what is wrong so as to avoid coming up with the energy needed for change. Obviously, if you're reading this book you're not one of these women—you're ready to take hold of what your life could be.

When you take action to change something, especially something as important as your life, there are risks. Creating new possibilities requires you to move outside your comfort zone, which very likely may be the cause of your discomfort in the first place. Replacing an ingrained habit with a new, healthier one can be painful at first. Stepping out on a new venture when the outcome is unknown can be scary. Changing the way you live can invite criticism from other people. Sadly, the potential cost, loss, or discomfort associated with taking risks prevents many people from moving off dead center.

• It's easier to sit on the sofa and watch TV than to get up, call your neighbor, and plan a time to walk two miles early tomorrow morning.

• It's easier to keep the job you dread every day than to explain your business plan to a banker in the commercial loan department.

• It's easier to put off making appointments for things you know you should do—get a mammogram or a physical; see your dentist to get your teeth cleaned—than to sit down with your calendar and schedule them.

• It's easier to pick up fat- and calorie-laden fast foods than to prepare fresh fruits and vegetables.

• It's easier to stay home and watch videos than to attend a book club, ballet, or symphony, where you might enhance yourself mentally and socially.

• It's easier to run the Sunday school class for five-year-olds than to admit to the friend who asked you to teach that you feel the need to attend an adult class where you can listen and learn.

• It's easier to keep traveling to your sister-in-law's for Thanksgiving and coming home exhausted than it is to tell her you and your family need some time alone this year.

Facing the Critics

I meet a lot of women who say that for them the hardest thing about taking a risk is the self-appointed discouragers in their lives.

Everybody's got at least one. It may be your mother, mother-in-law, father, spouse, boss, coworker—somebody who always sees what's wrong, never what could be right, with your ideas and aspira-

> "Change is not made without inconvenience, even from worse to better."   —Samuel Johnson

tions. Unfortunately, some
people in the world get a
kick out of making cynical
statements, cutting remarks,
and critical evaluations. They

> "All cruel people describe
> themselves as paragons of
> frankness!"
> —Tennessee Williams

seem to relish watching our countenance drop, our smile dissolve,
our energy dissipate, and our dreams die. In all fairness, a lot of
times these people don't really mean to be dream-killers. They live
in a small world and have a hard time seeing outside its boundaries. They can't imagine why anyone would want to risk making
a big change, taking on a challenge, or being a maverick or a
pioneer.

On the other hand, there are people who deliberately try to kill
others' dreams. Maybe they're jealous because they don't have
the courage to act on their own dreams. Maybe they're getting
even because someone squelched their dream. Many times criticism and cynicism are weapons in the arsenal of small people who
must attack others to maintain some degree of personal equilib-
rium. I am a woman with really big dreams and aspirations, and
I've had, and continue to have, plenty of criticism from people
who wonder who on earth I think I am trying to do some of the
things I do.

If you have dreams about personal success in one or more areas, and especially when you see your dreams becoming reality,
you can expect some criticism. But don't let this stop you. The
risks and costs of gaining the life you want and becoming the person you want to be are far less than the long-range risks and costs
of settling for a less-than-optimum life.

Be Smart about Change

Realize that your husband and children may not jump up and down at the thought of your making some changes. As a matter of fact, they may resist your changing. For example, if you decide to start cooking healthier so you and your family will feel better, your sixteen-year-old son who is addicted to junk food probably won't appreciate this change. If you decide to work out at the Y at 5:30 A.M. on weekdays, your husband may not like hearing the alarm go off at 4:45, even though he's glad you care about getting into shape. It's not that your son and husband don't want you to change; they're just concerned about how your changes will affect their world.

It is human nature to resist change, especially abrupt or forced change. We should put ourselves in the shoes of those affected by our changes and try to experience what they think and feel. Let's say you launch your new healthful-eating plan in a big way and immediately purge your kitchen of all products made from refined sugar or flour. You don't consider the fact that rice cakes and whole-wheat pretzels aren't exactly what your son and his football teammates are craving when they raid your pantry after practice.

Or maybe your husband is trying to finish a big project at work and must stay up late at night to meet a deadline. When your alarm goes off at 4:45 A.M., maybe he has had only three hours of sleep. Whatever the scenario, be considerate of the lives and schedules of others when making changes. Keep some teen-friendly snacks around and introduce new healthful options slowly. Put your alarm clock in the bathroom and be as quiet as a mouse when you get out of bed to turn it off and get dressed. Get your exercise clothes out the night before so you don't have to rummage through your drawers looking for your sports bra and a matching pair of socks.

Whatever the change you've decided to make in your life, in order to avoid or reduce the resistance of others, ask yourself these questions:

1. Who else will be affected by the change?
2. What reasons for resistance should I anticipate?
3. What methods can I use to introduce the change that will minimize their resistance?

Most people, whether family members or coworkers, accept change better if they are involved in the process; asked to contribute their feelings, opinions, and suggestions; and told the reasons for and advantages of a change.

THE BIGGEST CRITIC OF ALL

Dan Moore, a friend and colleague, introduced me to someone I had actually known for a long time; I just didn't know her name. Although I've spent a lot of time with her and listened to her comments over the years, I don't consider her my friend. As a matter of fact, she's my enemy, an uninvited guest in my life, and a pain to have around.

Whether or not you've been formally introduced, you know her, too. She treats you the same way she treats me. Her name is Ms. Mediocrity, and boy, does she have a mouth. She sits on your shoulder and mine and comments on our lives. She is especially vocal about anything that has to do with striving for excellence. As long as we're content to live a mediocre life, she leaves us alone. But the second we decide to make a change that will cause us to move in the direction of personal success, she camps out on our shoulder and talks nonstop into our ear. The dialogue goes something like this:

YOU: I'm tired of feeling run-down all the time. I'm going to make some changes in my life that will hopefully give my energy level a boost.

MS. M: Forget it—you can't change the way you are. Your mother said you've always moved slowly; your sister has all the energy.

YOU: I'll start by going to a health food store and buying some vitamins.

MS. M: That's a waste of money. You'll take them for a week and then they'll sit on the shelf until they get discolored.

YOU: I'll go to bed earlier, get up earlier, and start the day by walking around the block.

MS. M: You can't miss David Letterman. And please, do you *really* think you can get out of bed any earlier in the morning? You've tried that before, and it didn't work.

Sound familiar? More than likely you too have heard Ms. Mediocrity's voice on numerous occasions. In my opinion, she's much more dangerous to our success than a cynical friend. And she does a lot more damage than a critical mother-in-law. Ms. Mediocrity has meticulous files on every detail of your life. She's been especially careful to record the times you've failed, been embarrassed or rejected. She loves to remind you of these things.

She also loves comfort and ease. She balks at anything you think of doing that requires self-discipline. She generally hates change, unless, of course, you're backsliding or replacing a positive attitude or habit with something negative. Even something neutral will do for her purposes, just so you're not making strides toward success.

> "It is not the mountain we conquer but ourselves."
> —Sir Edmund Hillary

Ways to Tell We've Been Listening to Ms. M

- We feel a lack of self-confidence. Decisions feel bad even when they're good because we don't trust our own judgment.
- We feel like nothing is going right because nothing is perfect. Any little obstacle seems like a crisis.
- We snap at those we love.
- We make false assumptions about what others want and try to react to them.
- We eat or drink more than is good for us.
- We give up good exercise habits.
- We engage in a lot of negative self-talk such as "This is just the way I am" or "I just don't have what it takes."
- We feel sluggish and bored for no specific reasons.
- We think people are insincere when they pay us a compliment.
- We quit a project or learning endeavor that we started in enthusiasm.

DOING BATTLE WITH MS. M:
BELIEVING THE TRUTH ABOUT YOU

Unfortunately, you can't just flick Ms. M. off your shoulder once and for all. But you can limit the time she spends perched next to your ear and drown out her voice when she's speaking. There are specific actions you can take to maintain the frame of mind you need to live the life you really want and gain personal success.

All of us must understand one thing, and understand it thoroughly: how we see ourselves isn't necessarily based on facts. It's based on what we *believe* to be true. The way we see ourselves and what we think we can do and be—our self-image—develops over years of experiences, successes, and failures. It's reinforced each time we succeed or fail. It begins to develop when we are children and is influenced by how we think others see us, by what

> "We do not see things as they
> are. We see them as we are."
> —The Talmud

we think others expect of us, by what we imagine society expects of us, and by how we relate to others. No doubt about it: How we see ourselves is vitally important to our personal success and ability to take control of our life and change things.

When I was four years old, a playmate of mine scared me by telling me that the black spots in the center of bananas were crushed tarantula legs. From that day forth, I associated bananas with tarantulas. My subconscious stored untruths as facts. Our subconscious can't tell correct information from incorrect. It stores anything we tell it. Negative, destructive information will work through the subconscious into negative, destructive experiences. Positive, constructive information will work into positive, constructive experiences. For years, every time someone offered me a banana, my subconscious mind told me to not eat it. My conscious mind, on the other hand, knew that the black spots weren't tarantula legs.

We all hold certain beliefs about ourselves to be self-evident. Sometimes they're true. Sometimes they're not. Use the space provided in the box on page 47 to write down ten beliefs you hold about yourself and where you got them. Sometimes the source is pretty far back in your life. I have a friend nearing age fifty who, when pressed to come up with the source of her belief that she's not attractive, went all the way back to her childhood, when a relative said to her, "Your mother's so beautiful. And you look just like your aunt Mabel." Pretty slim evidence to base nearly half a century of belief on, isn't it? But we all do it.

> You and I are influenced more
> by what we think is so than
> what actually is so.

Take a moment right now to examine your own beliefs about yourself.

TEN BELIEFS I HOLD ABOUT MYSELF	HOW I GOT THEM	FACT OR FICTION?

1. _____

2. _____

3. _____

4. _____

5. _____

6. _____

7. _____

8. _____

9. _____

10. _____

Once you've got your list, go back over it and think hard. Is what you've listed really true? As you work on taking care of yourself, this is a list you might want to come back to. Have you listed characteristics you'd like to rid yourself of? Are there things you are ready to give up believing about yourself because they simply aren't true? Have you listed things you like about yourself? How can you use those strengths to your advantage? As you see yourself in a more positive light, you find a renewed sense of purpose, a new vitality, and a fresh agenda.

RESPONDING TO THE CRITICS

When someone, whether an outsider or ourselves, criticizes our efforts to change, it's easy to get discouraged and even give up. We lose the ability to think rationally about our situation. We begin negative self-talk: *She's right; it's a crazy idea.... I'll never change.... This is more than I can handle.... I really don't have what it takes.... Who am I to think I can succeed?*

When I feel discouraged I have a three-step response that I've found very helpful:

1. *Evaluate what is said.* Whatever the source, whatever the motive, there may be some truth in someone's discouraging words. Winston Churchill put it well: "The greatest lesson in life is to know that even fools can be right sometimes."

The way I see it, there's always room for improvement in what we're doing. Rather than wanting no critics, try to welcome their comments as a challenge to examine if you really believe in what you want to do.

2. *Affirm aloud to yourself what you know to be true.* Some years ago I hit a sad time, brought on by nothing I could put my finger on. The kids and Bill were doing fine. Things were hectic around our house, but no more so than usual. I realized I had been listening to Ms. M—believing her negative comments, which re-

> "If you're never scared or embarrassed or hurt, it means you never take chances."
> —Julia Sorel

sulted in a general sense of melancholy and a persistent feeling of defeat. I knew I needed to refocus my thoughts so I could get a clearer view of who I was and where I was going.

I discovered one thing I could do to reprogram my mind and emotions was to write and say to myself daily affirmations about who I am. I still often use them.

If that sense of sadness is familiar to you, perhaps you need to begin affirming the truth about yourself to yourself regularly, as I did. Let my affirmations help spark ideas for your own.

Who I Am

- I am a uniquely gifted, valuable person.
- I have a positive attitude toward life.
- I am tenacious.
- I am self-disciplined.
- I am continuously improving.
- I am honest and ethical.
- I am generous.
- I respond rather than react.
- I am a risk taker.
- I am a good-natured person, with a lively sense of humor.
- I am a person of high standards—I deliver more than I promise.
- I am a responsible person—I don't blame others for my mistakes.
- I am flexible.

- I am designed for a purpose. My skills and talents affirm this.
- I am loved more than I can imagine by God and others.

I am not by any stretch of the imagination all of these things. If I were, I wouldn't need the affirmations. But I find that repeating them helps convince my "down" self that I really am a valuable person, in ways that really count for me.

Take time soon to write your own affirmations. And keep in mind that your external performance is determined by your internal self-image. As you regularly affirm the positive qualities to which you aspire, your subconscious mind will accept these as commands and go to work to bring them into reality.

Use the following list for ideas:

friendly	thoughtful	good listener
honest	imaginative	energetic
dependable	organized	persistent
intelligent	successful	fun
creative	confident	loyal
flexible	patient	generous
loving	self-disciplined	empathetic
tenacious	strong	entertaining
helpful	gentle	responsible

3. *Let your progress speak for itself.* When you are attacked personally, defending yourself is of little value. And getting into a verbal fistfight accomplishes nothing positive. The best response to a critic or cynic is to let your progress and success speak for you. Let

"For as he thinks within himself, so he is."
—Proverbs 23:7

your cynical coworker see your newfound self-discipline when you grab your gym bag at lunchtime three days a week instead of watching soap operas in the employee lounge. Show your critical

> "I have oft regretted my speech—never my silence."
> —Publilius Syrus
>
> "When your work speaks for itself, don't interrupt."
> —Henry J. Kaiser

mother-in-law your report card along with your kids' report cards. Since you went back to college, although she thought it was a stupid idea, the kids are making As instead of Cs because you study together at night.

Growth Opportunity

Think of ways you might profit by taking risks in the following areas:

- Educational risks (taking a class outside your field; getting a degree; starting and leading a book club)
- Friendship risks (sharing feelings; dealing with unresolved conflict; making the first move to get to know someone)
- Spouse risks (sharing what you want, feel, or think; suggesting a change in the way you've divided up household responsibilities)
- Financial risks (deciding to get out of debt and cutting up your credit cards; investing; starting a new business)
- Physical risks (enrolling in a water-aerobics class; climbing a mountain; deciding to stop smoking)
- Material risks (purchasing a new car or house; simplifying your life—letting go of "excesses")
- Appearance risks (changing your hairstyle or color; getting makeup lessons from a professional cosmetologist; having braces put on your teeth)

- Emotional risks (making an appointment to talk about a problem with your pastor, rabbi, or counselor; taking an honest look at some unhealthy ways you express anger)
- Career risks (changing jobs; asking your boss for a more flexible schedule; seeking a promotion)

Overcoming Feeling Overwhelmed

Maybe you feel like you've got so many things you want to change about your life, you don't know where to start. You can't make yourself take the first step for fear it won't be the right one. A friend who feared making a lot of changes in her life told me it helped her immensely to think of herself as a tangled ball of yarn, rolled tightly in on herself. She said she knew that if she could untangle the yarn, she could weave a whole new piece of fabric. Yet she couldn't quite see how to untangle the yarn when she feared that pulling one strand would unravel the whole into a hopeless mess. She realized that taking that first small risk is like straightening out one bit of yarn. The more risks she takes, the more untangled yarn she has.

Sometimes our problems seem so interconnected that we can't see how to solve one without solving them all. We erroneously tell ourselves that until everything changes, nothing changes, so we risk nothing and resolve to live in our tangled state. Or we go to the opposite extreme and decide, come hell or high water, we're going to "risk the farm" and change everything—now. We throw caution to the wind and race from problem to problem, attempting to change everything and

> "There are risks and costs to a program of action, but they are far less than the long-range risks and costs of comfortable inaction."   —John F. Kennedy

thereby changing nothing. Either way, we're too overwhelmed to be effective.

> "Every noble work is at first impossible." —Thomas Carlyle

Maybe your life seems like my friend's knotty ball of yarn. If so, what one strand can you pull out right now?

CREATING AN AMBIANCE FOR CHANGE

Developing an atmosphere that allows us to make changes in our lives can in and of itself engender change. If I want to read on a regular basis so that I can be a better conversationalist, increase my intelligence, or just enjoy myself, the atmosphere I create—both internally and externally—contributes to my success or failure.

CREATING EXTERNAL ATMOSPHERE

- Select a cozy corner just for reading. Make sure it's comfortably furnished and has good light.
- Make sure there are times when your reading corner will be private and quiet.
- Read reviews for recommendations on what to read.
- Learn how to reserve books through your library; in some locations you can search for books and reserve them over the Internet. Check out used-book stores or budget funds for buying books each month.
- Write your reading "appointment" into your calendar.
- Create a ritual around reading. Choose a specific time of day—the hour before the kids get home or the hour after they go to bed, for example—for reading.
- Keep a reader's journal. Write down a quote from each book you read. Note the source of the quotes. (You'll track your progress and create a means of remembering what you read.)
- Start a readers' group with at least one friend. Meet monthly

to discuss your books. Join a book group at your library or bookstore.

- Ask for support from your husband. Be specific. Most men aren't mind readers. They don't know what we want unless we ask for it.

CREATING INTERNAL ATMOSPHERE

Internal atmosphere has a lot to do with attitude. We probably all fit somewhere on a continuum between Nancy Never Happen and Carol Can Do. If you find that you're dwelling on the pitfalls, obstacles, and setbacks, feeling like the change will never really be integrated into your life, you're probably going to need to get support for your new process. Reading with a friend falls into both the external and the internal categories. You might put notes around the house where you'll see them frequently to remind yourself why you're doing this.

If you're having trouble sticking to a reading program, you might ask yourself why. Are there beliefs you hold about yourself that aren't really facts? Does part of you believe you're not smart enough to engage in a discussion about a book? Do you think that reading is a way of avoiding what you should be doing or that you don't deserve time to yourself to read? Maybe, for example, your job requires that you read a lot of technical material. Sure, you'd love to read a novel for pleasure or an inspirational book for self-improvement, but when you have time to yourself, books just aren't appealing because of the overkill at work. Still, you have this dream of personal success in this area. Maybe you need to consider listening to books on tape or to take turns reading chapters out loud with a friend or your husband. Often there are ways around the obstacles you perceive.

> Fact: It takes twenty-one repetitions to change a habit.

Sometimes when we try to form new habits, a feeling of deprivation sneaks in. The most obvious example I can think of is when we try to

> "You can't break a bad habit by throwing it out the window. You've got to walk it slowly down the stairs." —Mark Twain

lose weight. Almost everybody who sets out on a weight-loss and exercise program experiences a feeling of deprivation. Despite the fact that you are losing weight and/or getting into better shape and that your clothes fit better, Ms. Mediocrity rears her ugly head and whispers things like: "Oh, poor you. You'll never eat a chocolate sundae again." "You're always going to feel hungry." "What are you going to do when you're sad if you don't let yourself have those cookies you usually eat?" Her voice is not going to go away, but you can drown her out if you remind yourself of the benefits of what you're doing.

NO WOMAN IS AN ISLAND

Let's be honest: it's easier to accomplish tasks in teams. Strength or willpower naturally increases with numbers. Here's a case in point: I have the tendency occasionally to graze—to eat standing up. It's easy to forget about the calories or fat grams I consume in this way. I've learned to let James, our youngest son, hold me accountable: if he sees me eating standing up, he gets to fine me one dollar. He loves this moneymaking project, and I love adhering to my food plan.

Whenever you commit to do something, small or large, short- or long-term, it never hurts and often helps to convey your plan to those around you. Your family and trusted friends and advisers can see your vision from a different vantage point. They can often help

> "Any two of us are smarter than any one of us."
> —Wayne Paulson

us figure out what to do and how to do it. If we listen to them, they can also help us avoid the pitfalls of overcommitment.

An accountability buddy, someone who is committed to your success, can be a coach and a cheerleader to inspire you when you're flagging. Plus, sharing your progress and your shortfalls can help you to be honest with yourself; you will then be more likely to follow through.

HITTING ROUGH PATCHES

When I'm having trouble integrating an action plan into my life, I do two things. First, I go back and review my vision. Is it still what I really want? Or does my evaluation and analysis of what should be done need fine-tuning?

Obstacles to Action Plans

1. *Unrealistic expectations.* Who among us is not sometimes guilty of having unrealistic expectations? Perhaps the problem is not an unreasonable goal, but unreasonable timing, like losing thirty pounds before a reunion that's coming up in two months.

2. *Flagging commitment.* Again, this could have to do with timing. Am I trying to do it all too fast? Sometimes we have to give new habits time to become second nature before we can build on them. I may also need to examine what is getting in the way of my commitment. Are there ways to rearrange my life so that I can meet my vision of my personal best?

3. *Judging ourselves.* When we're having trouble moving forward, it may be time to offer ourselves some compassion. How are we motivating ourselves? Are we telling ourselves that we're bad if we don't continue with a reasonable daily action plan? Are we trying to use fear on ourselves? Are we saying, "If I don't lose some weight and get into shape I'm going to drop dead or lose my husband"? Most of us would not try to motivate our children to

change by using these tac-
tics, yet we often persist in
using versions of them on
ourselves. We need to give
them up. They don't work,
and they're unkind.

> "A problem well stated is a
> problem half solved."
> —Charles F. Kettering

When you encounter an obstacle to doing what you want to do,
try to discover what's stopping you.

Five Steps to Obstacle Removal

When something stands in the way of your goal, go through these
steps to see the problem dissolve.

1. Visualize the need clearly in your mind. Dispense with any
   added-on problems or things you can't control. Look at the obstacle for what it is.
2. Take your brain out of edit mode. Don't assign limitations. Let
   creativity operate.
3. Jot down ideas on paper. You never know which seed of an idea
   will sprout. Keep the ideas—even if they're just doodles.
4. Let one idea lead to another. Don't let frustration over the
   problem stymie your thinking. Two heads are better than one.
   Ask a friend to brainstorm with you.
5. Take a risk. Do a little something. A first step leads to a second
   and so forth.
6. The key is to start moving. Think of it like this: it's easier to
   steer a moving car than a parked one. That's a simple principle
   of physics. It's also not a bad principle to live by. Whether it's
   finishing that degree, setting up a single moms' support group,
   getting a promotion at work, or carving out time to nourish
   friendships.

> "Behold the turtle. He makes progress only when he sticks his neck out."
> —James Bryant Conant

> "Challenges make you discover things about yourself that you never really knew. They're what make the instrument stretch— what make you go beyond the norm."
> —Cicely Tyson

INNOVATION TURNS PROBLEMS INTO OPPORTUNITIES

I am inspired by the stories of people who turn problems into opportunities. History is full of examples of people who didn't take no for an answer. Wilma Rudolph ("Limpy" is what her classmates called her) was born with one leg shorter than the other and became an Olympic gold medalist in track and field. George Eliot (real name: Mary Ann Evans) was over forty when she published her first novel. Alexander Fleming searched for ten years for a pharmaceutical company that would fund his idea for penicillin.

What obstacles are keeping you from moving toward personal success? What one thing can you do today to get around an obstacle?

ATTITUDE ADJUSTMENTS

None of us can control all of our circumstances. But we can always control our attitude—which may be even more powerful. My friend Mary Bailey knows about the power of attitude from the inside out. Born with one leg shorter than the other, early on she faced limitations and the unpleasant reality of wearing an awkward-looking three-inch lift on her shoe. Mary describes the day her parents brought home the lift. She was five and she knew ugly when she saw it. "I remember being really angry and throwing that shoe on the ground," she recalls. "I ran upstairs and got into my

> "In the middle of difficulty lies opportunity."
> —Albert Einstein

closet." There, even as a kindergartner, Mary made peace with her situation. "I thought, *If this is what it's going to take for me to get better, to be okay, then I'm going to do it. I'm not going to complain about it.* I remember feeling totally peaceful. That attitude carried over when this other, bigger tragedy came along."

> "Nothing splendid has ever been achieved except by those who dared believe that something inside them was superior to circumstances."
> —Bruce Barton

Mary refers to her bout with Guillain-Barré syndrome, a postviral infection that felled her at age eleven. Her arms and legs were paralyzed for almost a year, and Mary was confined to a wheelchair for the duration. Yet her positive mind-set made her envision the best possible scenario: "For a long time, I just assumed I would get over it completely," she says. "Slowly it dawned on me over the years that wasn't happening. That was very disheartening," she admits. "But I made a conscious choice to focus on the positive instead of the negative."

And Mary did progress; eventually her paralysis extended only to her feet. She graduated from clunky metal braces in junior high to ankle-foot orthotics, knee-high contraptions that kept (and keep) her off the track and out of high heels. Yet she played on her high school's basketball team for two years—until, as she said, "I realized that someone who can't run that fast and can't jump doesn't really need to be playing basketball." Mary concentrated on her other gifts—good friends, a sharp mind, encouraging parents—and did what everybody else did most of the time: "Sometimes I just needed a little more help.

"Everybody has something they don't like about themselves—you can become really depressed by it," she says today. "I could have become a hermit. I could have imposed limits on myself because I was self-conscious or angry, but what good does that do?

> "Let not your mind run on what you lack as much as on what you have already."
> —Marcus Aurelius

Then you miss all these other wonderful things." Some of the wonderful things Mary has experienced are marriage (to a physical therapist!) and motherhood. The key to her attitude, she says, is her realization that for every activity she couldn't do, there were many more she could. She focuses on those she can do.

Ways to Improve Your Attitude and Chances for Success

- Know what you want to achieve, from getting a teaching certificate to consistently doing a monthly breast self-examination. Take the time to decide if what you think you want is really what you want.
- Be patient. Incremental progress is still progress, so reward yourself accordingly. Realize that progress does not mean perfection. Don't let three steps forward and two steps back get you down.
- Be willing to sacrifice. If you need some quiet, personal time to start your day on a peaceful note, get up an hour earlier to read a chapter of an inspirational book and spend time in prayer and meditation.
- Know your strengths and limitations. Turn down requests and opportunities that don't make the best use of your abilities. Know how to say yes and no in accordance with the priorities and values you hold. Limitations are not faults; a body of water without limits can turn into a swamp.
- Be a perpetual learner. Ask lots of questions and stay alert to new ideas and techniques wherever they appear. Try to learn

something from everyone—mentors, friends, kids, and the clerk at the corner store.

- Practice serenity in the midst of chaos. Don't let yourself be easily rattled or shaken by negative circumstances or difficult situations.
- Be resilient. Listen to and honestly assess the criticism of others. Some of it is valid and useful.
- Spend time getting to know your strengths and weaknesses. Accept them both.

The Bottom Line

- People who risk nothing may think they are avoiding suffering and sorrow, but they cannot learn, feel, change, grow, love, or really live. Chained by their attitudes, they are slaves; they have forfeited their freedom. Only a person who risks is free.
- Having an accurate picture of your value and potential is the driving force behind any changes you want to see in yourself.
- How we see ourselves isn't necessarily based on facts; it's based on what we believe to be true. It's important to regularly read aloud your personal affirmations.
- You can't completely silence Ms. Mediocrity, but you can take positive action to limit her influence.
- Don't fear change. It can lead you to a better place.
- Be willing to risk: it separates the women from the girls, the doers from the whiners, and the explorers from the daydreamers. See it as the key to making your desires come to fruition.
- Developing an atmosphere that allows us to make changes in our lives can in and of itself engender change.
- Don't be surprised if you find that as you accomplish the items on your list, you have renewed energy and enthusiasm.

I encourage you to start today. Take a risk. As you begin to step out toward the dreams you have for yourself, you'll find a renewed sense of purpose, a new vitality, and fresh courage to take the next steps. Know that it's better to try and fail than not to try at all. You'll find that the rewards greatly outweigh the risks.

FOUR

Finding Time for You

"Guard well your spare moments. They are like uncut diamonds. Improve them and they will become the brightest gems in a useful life."　　　　　—Ralph Waldo Emerson

I'm going to make a bold assertion: finding time to do what we want to do is as simple as one, two, three:

One, identify the time robbers in our lives.

Two, get rid of them.

Three, replace them with actions and activities that reflect the changes we want to make in our lives.

Note I said *simple*. I didn't say *easy*. It's not easy to say no to a friend who wants you to commit three hours a day for the next month to help run a bazaar to earn money for a children's hospital. It's not easy to get up an hour earlier in the morning to have time to study for a graduate-level course. It's not easy to decide between seeing a movie with a friend and spending a few hours alone on the rare weekend when the kids are at camp and your husband is on a business trip. It's not easy to turn down a promotion at the office that would mean more interesting work—and longer hours and more travel. And there is no one right way to handle any of these dilemmas or opportunities. But there is an answer, and that is that

> "Time is the coin of your life. It is the only coin you have, and only you can determine how it will be spent. Be careful lest you let other people spend it for you."   —Carl Sandburg

each of us needs to make choices—on a daily basis.

All of us can learn to iden-tify the things that eat up our time and can make plans and choices to minimize the effects of time robbers.

Sixty-nine Minutes and Counting

Just how easily time slips through our fingers became apparent to me when a bookstore manager told me a story about a friend she invited to a Family Manager workshop at her store. An hour before the workshop was to begin, the friend telephoned. It took her twenty minutes to explain in detail that she'd had a run-behind day and couldn't make it.

First, she lost her car keys. She was ten minutes late for work. Then when she got to the bank at lunchtime, she discovered she'd forgotten to put the check she planned to deposit in her purse. Late in the afternoon, she realized that she had no clue what she would fix for dinner, so she had to stop at the grocery store on the way home, at peak time, and wander around until she figured out what she could cook quickly. By the time she got home, sorted the groceries, and started to cook dinner, she was exhausted and out of time, not to mention worried that her checks would bounce be-cause she hadn't made her deposit. She couldn't possibly get to a workshop to learn how to save time and minimize stress. So she called her friend and talked for twenty minutes instead.

If she'd come that night, she might well have been too stressed to benefit from the workshop. But let's add up the time she could have saved during the day:

- A hook she always hung her car keys on could have saved ten minutes of search time.
- A shelf or table next to the door where she always put things she needed to take with her when she left for the day could have saved fifteen minutes, a fruitless trip to the bank, and a lot of frustration.
- If she had planned out her menus and started dinner in the morning—maybe by doing something as simple as putting chicken breasts with barbecue sauce in the slow cooker— she could have saved the twenty-five minutes wasted by the trip to the store.
- If she hadn't felt the need to take twenty minutes to explain the ins and outs of her day to her friend, she could have made a one-minute call, saying simply, "Sorry, I can't make it." Nineteen more minutes lost.

By my count, that's sixty-nine minutes, or exactly enough to make the ten-minute drive to and from her house to the forty-five-minute seminar, with four minutes left over to walk from and to the parking lot.

Identifying Time Robbers

Recently Bill and I had dinner with a couple who told us a frightening story about being robbed. While they were sleeping, a man broke into their home and slipped quietly from room to room searching for valuables. When he entered the oldest daughter's room, she woke up. He ordered her to not move or make a sound. Finally, when she sensed he was out of the house, she ran screaming into her parents' bedroom. They called

> "Our costliest expenditure is time."   —Theophrastus

> "Time flies over us, but leaves
> its shadow behind."
> —Nathaniel Hawthorne

the police, who came immediately and searched the area. One of the officers suggested some defensive strategies to help the family members protect themselves against future break-ins: better locks on the doors, bright outside floodlights, an alarm system. He also outlined other ways to foil professional thieves.

Each and every one of us is robbed of something very valuable every day, and it's taken right from under our noses. We're robbed of our time. The culprits aren't burglars or muggers, although they may be people who consciously or unconsciously take our time. The most common culprits are circumstances, daily activities, and ourselves.

We've all had the experience of not knowing where the time goes. We're being robbed, but we don't know who or what is robbing us. I've discovered that knowing how our time is spent helps enormously in using our time for our own best purposes. So periodically I keep track. I use a small notebook with enough space to write things down. I'm looking for ways I spend my time, but I'm especially looking for ways I spend my time that aren't part of my agenda or my life as I want it to be. If my book is at hand, I'm more likely to note everything down and not conveniently forget that I spent two hours on the phone talking to two friends and my mother about nothing in particular. Now I'm not saying it's necessarily a bad thing to spend time on the phone with friends and family. But in order to make time for ourselves, we need to note and evaluate how much time we spend doing what in any given day.

Here are some things to pay attention to:

- What time do you get out of bed?
- How much alone time do you have before your family gets up?

- How much time do you spend getting dressed for the day?
- What do you do when the kids leave for school?
- What do you do while commuting to and from work?
- Small tasks and large projects during the day—how long do you spend on them? Are they finished when you're done?
- Phone calls—how many, how long, and what are they about?
- Shopping and errands—when you go, how long does it take?
- What are the lengths of your breaks and lunchtime?
- When and how long do you watch TV?
- When and how long do you clean house and do the laundry?
- What or who interrupts you?
- How much time do you spend searching for misplaced items?
- What and when do you read?
- How much time do you spend exercising?
- When do you go to the grocery store?
- How much time do you spend fixing meals and eating?
- How much time do you spend with your kids and/or spouse? Doing what?
- How much time do you spend shopping?
- How much time do you spend standing in lines?
- Do you bring work home from the office, and how long do you spend on it?
- What time do you go to bed?
- How long does it take you to fall asleep?
- How much time do you spend praying, meditating, or just staring at the sky?

After a week, you'll have a pretty good record of how you spend your time and energy and who your robbers are. The next step is to evaluate your journal so you can begin to put into practice better ways of taking care of yourself.

How much time did you spend doing things not on your daily

to-do list? Which of those things depleted your energy and robbed you of time to do things you wanted to do? Which of those things could have been left undone, postponed, or delegated to someone else?

Make a list of the things you're *not* going to do in the next week. It's a step toward getting rid of time robbers. This list might include watching television, listening to your sister-in-law complain on the phone, saying yes to anyone who calls for anything, or doing your teenager's laundry.

This is simply another way to focus on your time and how you spend it. I've found that for some people this can also be an attitude check. Is it really as depleting as I think it is to cook dinner? Would planning menus and shopping ahead make it more rewarding? How about trading with a coworker? You cook double twice a week, she cooks double twice a week, you bring the extra portion to each other at work in a cooler. Results: You both get two nights off a week from cooking. Would playing your favorite music or working with your kids make it more rewarding? What else might?

Here's a list of fifty-four things that might be robbing you of time. Check the ones that apply to you and consider implementing the time-saver tip.

Time-Robber Chart

TIME ROBBERS	TIME SAVERS
1. Trying to decide what to do first	Use a Daily Hit List (see page 83) to order your day.
2. Fixing and refixing your hair	Get a hairstylist to give you a good cut that's easy to manage.
3. Answering unimportant phone calls	Screen your calls with caller ID, an answering machine, or voice-mail service.

TIME ROBBERS	TIME SAVERS
4. Reading unimportant e-mails	Delete junk e-mail before opening it.
5. Searching for panty hose without runs	Purchase panty hose in bulk three or four times a year when they're on sale. Keep hose with runs that you can wear under pants in a separate plastic bag or bin.
6. Looking for your car keys	Put a hook by your exit door and start the habit of hanging your keys on the hook right when you walk in the door.
7. Helping your child look for lost school papers, permission forms, etc.	Create in-boxes for each family member. Have kids unload backpacks after school and put important papers in their in-box.
8. Picking up clutter	Create Clutter Jail. When family members leave their belongings out, put the items in a box or crate. Have the culprits post bail to retrieve their belongings.
9. Surfing the Internet	Do you really need the information or item you're looking for? Keep a kitchen timer by your computer to help you keep track of how long you've spent on-line.
10. Sorting through junk mail	Use cardboard magazine holders to create a family mail center. Personalize a holder for each individual and have one for catalogs and magazines. Place a trash can nearby. Toss junk mail immediately as you sort the rest.

TIME ROBBERS	TIME SAVERS
11. Buying last-minute birthday gifts	Keep a few generic gifts on hand (picture frames, candles, books, etc.). Gift certificates to toy or sports stores and theaters are also good.
12. Running to the ATM machine to get cash	Withdraw all the cash you will need for the week or the month at one time. Keep in an envelope in a secure place.
13. Coping with kids who dawdle in the morning	Create a no-play-until-ready rule. Turn off the television.
14. Making last-minute transportation arrangements for kids' activities	Arrange all necessary transportation as early as possible, at least the day before.
15. Hunting for an article or recipe in a magazine you read last month	When you read an article or recipe in a magazine or newspaper that you want to keep, tear it out and stick it in a large envelope until you have time to file it in the appropriate place.
16. Fixing breakfast and cleaning up afterward	Set the table and do as many preparations as you can the night before. Offer a very limited menu of easy-to-prepare but healthy foods. Divide preparation and cleanup chores between family members.
17. Backtracking when you run errands	Before you run errands, write down everywhere you need to go and plan the most expeditious route.
18. Figuring out what to wear and which accessories look good	Decide the night before what you will wear and how best to accessorize. Have your kids do this, too. (Be sure to check for missing buttons, spots, and sagging hemlines.)

TIME ROBBERS	TIME SAVERS
19. Taking back an overdue video at a nonoptimum time	Rewind videos immediately after watching. Put them on a shelf or in an errand basket by the exit door.
20. Searching for office supplies at home—stamps, rubber bands, paper clips, etc.	Set up a Control Central that includes a mini–home office and an ample amount of basic office supplies.
21. Nagging family members	Call a family meeting and create house rules everyone can live with. Have consequences for noncooperation.
22. Playing referee for disgruntled siblings	Make sure your house rules cover things like sharing toys, time spent at the computer, etc.
23. Looking for the mates to socks, shoes, or gloves	Have kids pick up all belongings before bed. Then have them set out all clothing and gear the night before.
24. Making a special trip to buy wrapping paper for gifts	Set up a wrapping station in a large drawer or portable plastic crate and keep it stocked with various kinds of wrapping paper, ribbon, tape, scissors, gift bags, and tags.
25. Running to the grocery store for one ingredient you need for a recipe	Plan menus ahead and write down all ingredients needed. Keep your pantry well stocked.
26. Going to the post office each time you need to mail a small package	Set up a mailing center in your home. Include a small postal scale, various denominations of stamps, boxes, different sizes of envelopes and padded mailers, and a postal rate chart.

TIME ROBBERS	TIME SAVERS
27. Going to the bank to make deposits	Set up automatic deposit through your employer. Or have a set time once a week when you go to the bank. Avoid Fridays.
28. Ironing because the clothes sat in the dryer too long	As soon as the clothes are done in the dryer, fold them or hang them up. Teach kids this habit early.
29. Agreeing to hold on the telephone while waiting for someone	While you're waiting multitask and get something else done: balance your checkbook, clean out your purse, declutter a drawer, dust a shelf.
30. Driving during high-traffic times of day	Avoid running errands during the lunch hour or five o'clock rush hour. Shopping right when stores open or right before they close is usually faster.
31. Procrastinating	Decide to do something (even if it's something small) every day toward accomplishing projects you've let pile up.
32. Waiting at appointments	Always be prepared to accomplish something if you think you'll have to wait. Take a book, some notepaper, or needlework. Call ahead to see if the person you're meeting is running on schedule.
33. Chatting on the phone with long-winded friends	Call long-winded friends before you need to leave to go somewhere or accomplish a task. This way you have a legitimate exit from the phone call.

TIME ROBBERS	**TIME SAVERS**
34. Waiting to wash dishes until they're caked with dried-on food	Have a house rule that you clean dishes immediately after eating. If that's not possible, fill the sink with hot soapy water and soak the dishes.
35. Stopping at the grocery store on the way home from work	Plan menus during the weekend for the coming week. Shop once a week at a less crowded time (late at night or early in the morning).
36. Not putting things back where they belong	Create a family policy to not put things down, but to put them away after using.
37. Looking up frequently called phone numbers again and again	Create a family yellow pages, which lists all of your family's frequently called numbers. Keep a highlighter pen near your phone book and mark other numbers you call.
38. Not keeping party invitation information handy so you have to call to find out details	Keep all party invitations filed in a central location. Write locations and phone numbers on your calendar.
39. Making an extra trip back home or to school because you or your child forgot something	Have children load their backpacks the night before. Put everything you need to take— purse, briefcase, errand items— near the exit door.
40. Searching for pens or pencils that actually work	Keep all office supplies at your Control Central station. Purge it regularly of any pens that don't work. (This is a good task for kids.)
41. Returning items to a store for credit	Buy only things you know you want. Don't buy impulsively.

TIME ROBBERS	TIME SAVERS
42. Nervous snacking	Be alert for times that you eat because you're nervous, not because you're hungry. Drink a big glass of water instead. And don't eat standing up; remember, cows graze.
43. Feeling so overwhelmed with too much to do that you end up not doing anything	Always ask, "Can this task be delegated to someone else?" Try to do only what you can do.
44. Getting lost driving around because you don't have directions or a map	Keep a map in the glove compartment of your car. Write down the address and phone number of the place you're going before you leave.
45. Writing the same information over and over— babysitter instructions, grocery lists, medical emergency releases, travel lists	Create forms for babysitter instructions, grocery lists, medical emergency releases, etc. (If you don't have a computer and printer, handwrite the forms and have them duplicated at a printing center.)
46. Not having an extra key to your house and car readily accessible	Always keep an extra key to your house hidden outside and an extra car key in your purse or calendar notebook.
47. Whining about how little time you have	Stop whining. It accomplishes nothing.
48. Dwelling on failures you can't do anything about	Remember that everyone makes mistakes. Learn from what you did, and move on.
49. Not having necessary cleaning supplies on hand	Make a list of what cleaning supplies you need at the first of every month and then buy them. Have a family rule that when you use up a product, you write it down on the grocery list.

TIME ROBBERS	TIME SAVERS
50. Picking up multipiece toys	Keep a clean dustpan in your child's room to scoop up toys.
51. Storing things you use regularly in out-of-the-way places	Check to see if you're taking up prime storage space with any items that you don't use frequently. Replace with more frequently used things.
52. Packing toiletries in an overnight bag every time you travel	Purchase travel-size items/bottles for all your toiletries and keep them in an overnight bag.
53. Not requiring kids to help with housework	Have a rule at your house that kids do not get their privileges— watching TV, playing computer games, talking on the phone— until they fulfill their responsibilities. Stand firm.
54. Watching TV	Limit television viewing to programs that are really worth your time. Accomplish something productive while watching television—fold laundry, exercise, dust furniture, polish shoes, brush the dog or cat.

Remember, finding time for ourselves isn't going to happen instantaneously. It takes being alert for the things that are robbing us of time, and then being sure to fill that time with more meaningful activities.

Maybe when you tracked your time you learned that, like the average American, the television is on in your home more than three hours a day. TV might be robbing you of time in other places as well. This point was illustrated recently

"Lost time is never found again."   —Benjamin Franklin

when I presented a Family Manager seminar to a group of working mothers at a large corporation. A couple of them complained to me that they just didn't have time to plan menus ahead. So they picked up fast food many more nights than they liked to admit. Nor did they have time to exercise. They left the house when their kids did in the morning, and at night they were too tired or had too many other things to do.

The seminar was right before lunch. Afterward, I was taken on a tour of the plant. In the employee lunchroom, those same women were glued to the TV, watching their daily soap opera. Here we identified a time robber. I suggested that they could tape this show at home and use their lunch hour to brainstorm menus with coworkers. Or they could go to the employee gym to exercise. Again, there's no right or wrong way to spend a lunch hour. But wouldn't it be great to use that time to accomplish some of your goals? Being alert for time robbers is another way to keep more time for ourselves.

The Best Defense Is a Good Defense *and* a Good Game Plan

I recently met Julie, a family manager with three children whose everyday schedule would make most of us tired. Coping with her job as family manager was wearing Julie out far more than her demanding job as a gift-store manager. Here's the scene: every night Mom and Dad arrive home from work about seven o'clock. Between then and putting the kids to bed at eight-thirty, they need to decide what to have for dinner—which four nights out of five means running out to the store or eating takeout they've picked up on the way home. (It's a pattern Julie dislikes, as takeout is expensive and usually high in fat.) Then they do homework with the six-year-old and the nine-year-old while the two-year-old runs nearly constant interference. Then laundry and housework have to get done—and Mom does most of it. In addition, both parents are enrolled in college classes and volunteer about fifteen hours a week at their church.

When I first started working with them, I asked them what their children were going to grow up remembering about home. I suggested that their home resembled a fast-food restaurant in which everyone rushed in and grabbed a bite. The rest of the evening was like a home movie in fast-forward: the kids hurriedly doing their homework, their little brother running about causing trouble, and Mom racing around doing housework. What kinds of memories are those?

As we talked, I also asked Julie about her work. Instead of her wasting half an hour running to the store four nights a week, I suggested she plan ahead just as she does at work so that she has the right stock on hand for upcoming holidays and seasonal events. I asked her what happens when there are three customers in the store and only one clerk. Does she constantly interrupt herself with one to talk to the other? Or does she invite two to browse while she aids the first one? Maybe she could create a "homework box" filled with coloring books, crayons, and small toys to amuse her two-year-old so he doesn't distract her from time with her older children. Or maybe the nine-year-old could read a book aloud to the youngest while Julie helps her six-year-old with spelling words.

To look beyond the daily, I suggested that Julie and her husband examine each activity in their lives and ask themselves if it's really what they want to be doing. School may be important to both of them, but perhaps they should consider going one at a time. Maybe they could change their volunteer roles at the church so they're spending time with at least one of their kids while they work, or maybe they could recruit more volunteers to share the work. Maybe they could divide up household chores between themselves and the two older children. Maybe housekeeping standards could be lowered. Maybe Julie needs to find half an hour or an hour once a week in which she has time for herself so she'll survive this overly busy season of her life.

Let me add a quick confession here lest I sound like I consider myself superior to this woman and her household struggles: the only reason I have suggestions for someone like Julie is because I've been Julie. I know what it's like to try to split my time between a job I needed, a family I loved, and volunteer work I cared about. The family management strategies I shared with Julie I learned the hard way.

Did you know that every time you get interrupted it takes three minutes to get back on track? If you've got a project to finish, screen your calls. Leave a note on your office door asking people to write a message and saying you'll get back to them at a specific time. Even young children can be taught that you'll get back to them in twenty minutes, especially if you promise to read them a favorite book or play a game when you've finished what you need to do. When my boys were preschool age I kept a box of special toys and activities on my closet shelf, which I got down only when I needed to buy a bit of time to do something.

In order to find time for ourselves, we have to identify time robbers for what they are and figure out how to keep them out of our houses and our lives. We also need to have a good game plan, to know what's important to us, and to stick to it. Rigorously.

> "Lost, yesterday, somewhere between sunrise and sunset, two golden hours, each set with sixty diamond minutes. No reward is offered, for they are gone forever."
>
> —Horace Mann

Finding Hidden Treasure

There was a time in my life when I lived on a treadmill. I had set my priorities and goals, and I knew what I wanted to accomplish in a given day or week. I was even careful to schedule time for exercise and reading for myself. I listed the tasks on a sheet of paper and posted it in an easy-to-see location. I even placed a pen nearby so I could cross items off the list as I accomplished them. But I wasn't crossing off much. At the end of the week, instead of feeling good about all I had done, I felt guilty about what I hadn't.

Each week I would try again, and each week I couldn't figure out where my time had gone and why I couldn't get much done. My load of guilt kept getting heavier and heavier. I felt as if I were being cheated, robbed of time I could ill afford to lose. Then I learned an important lesson about time management from my youngest son. (I don't know about you, but I think one of the greatest—and least acknowledged—benefits of being a parent is what we learn from our kids.)

Our son James has an uncanny ability to find money in random, obscure places. When we walk by pay telephones or drink machines, he runs his finger through the change slots and often finds treasure. At baseball games he checks under the bleachers and comes up with cash. We'll be having a picnic—throwing the Frisbee, eating potato salad and chicken, swatting at mosquitoes—and James will be doing everything we're doing. Plus he'll be scanning the grass for change people have dropped. He gives new meaning to the term *pay dirt*. Once at a park cabin he found a twenty-dollar bill behind a sofa pillow.

Because he expects to, James finds opportunities that others miss. He's paying attention. He doesn't find money every time, but he finds it a lot more frequently because he looks for it.

It occurred to me that I could learn a lesson from him: I could start looking at time as treasure and be alert for situations in which I might find it. I thought about how and why James finds money. He isn't any luckier than the rest of us. He doesn't have some built-in radar that leads him directly to coins or green paper. He is simply focused on his goal—to find money. It's not all-consuming. He's got numerous other responsibilities, activities, and interests. But part of his brain is always aware of his goal.

So I made my goal finding time to do the things I needed and wanted to do. I didn't give up on making lists. But I did give up considering myself a failure if I didn't check off everything on them. I gently reminded myself of my goal: to find the time to do the things I wanted to do. And after a while, I began to see the possibilities.

When people want to know how I do all that I do, I tell them it's a direct result of being alert and paying attention—locating five minutes here, ten minutes there, thirty minutes now and then—and using whatever time I find to accomplish something. I've learned never to underestimate the potential of snippets of time.

In one recent day, I found at least two hours. I edited a chapter while I waited forty-five minutes to see the doctor, who was running late. Since I'm on deadline, I knew that I'd deplete my energy even more by fuming if I hadn't had something to work on. I found fifteen more minutes by asking James to start dinner while I returned two phone calls. (In those two calls, I found another fifteen minutes by telling a colleague I couldn't chat just then because James was waiting for me to help him finish dinner.) I found an hour by getting Joel, who was at home for another few weeks before he returned to college, to run some errands with me. By going to the mall together, we accomplished a lot—not the least of which was spending that time together in the car talking. If I'd gone to the mall alone it could easily have taken me two hours, and I wouldn't have spent time with my son.

A Practical Way
to Accomplish More Each Day

If you've read any of my other books about family management, you know that I'm a big believer in using a Daily Hit List, which is different from a typical to-do list. A Hit List brings sense to your day by categorizing your myriad chores in the seven departments you oversee in your home:

Home and Property—overseeing the maintenance and care of all your tangible assets, including personal belongings and the house and its surroundings

Food—efficiently, economically, and creatively meeting the daily food and nutrition needs of your family

Time—managing time and schedules—getting the right people to the right places at the right time—so that your household can run smoothly

Finances—managing budgets, bill paying, saving, investing, and other money issues

Special Projects—coordinating large and small projects (birthdays, holidays, vacations, garage sales, family reunions) that fall outside your normal family routine

Family Members and Friends—dealing with family life and relationships, and acting as teacher, nurse, counselor, mediator, and social chairman; keeping up your end of your marriage

Personal Management—growing and caring for yourself physically, emotionally, intellectually, and spiritually

> "Dost thou love life? Then do not squander time, for that's the stuff life is made of."
> —Benjamin Franklin

Listing what needs to be done each day by department will allow you to see more clearly what needs to be accomplished.

After you list the day's tasks in their appropriate department, you can apply the Three-D strategy:

1. D*elete.* See if there are some chores you can scratch off your list. Do you really need to dust the living room? Just because your mother dusted every Monday and Thursday doesn't mean you have to.

2. D*elegate.* Look at your Hit List and see what chores you can assign to other family members. Remember, "women's work" went out with girdles. At our house the men can cook, sew, and clean just as well as I can—and sometimes better. And I can mow the yard, paint, and use a hammer. Everyone who lives under the roof of the house should participate in the upkeep of the house.

3. D*o.* What do *you* need to do? Many women make use of a Hit List to note crucial things: "Laundry," "Send Aunt Sue a birthday card," or "Shop for groceries." But they fail to see the importance of listing tasks that help them reach their personal best. "Look up remedies for PMS" or "Take a two-mile walk" or "Schedule appointment for a makeup consultation" should be just as important as any other item on the list.

I think you'll find that by using the Three-D strategy with a Daily Hit List you'll accomplish more and have more time for taking care of you.

Spending Treasure Wisely

As I write this, I know full well how I need to follow my own advice. It's summer, always a busy time for a family manager. The memory

DAILY HIT LIST™

DATE: 3-1

SCHEDULE	HOME & PROPERTY	FOOD	FAMILY & FRIENDS
5:00 _____	Dry cleaners	Dinner	Call Mother
6:00 work out		BBQ	
7:00 _____	Get bid on new roof	chicken corn	Research music
8:00 James to school		salad	teachers
9:00 _____	Plant pansies	fruit	for James
10:00 _____	Change sheets	Take Lynn chicken soup and get-well card	Send Jean a birthday card
11:00 _____			
NOON Lunch w/Peggy			
1:00 _____			
2:00 _____			

SCHEDULE	FINANCES	SPECIAL PROJECTS	PERSONAL
3:00 _____	Pay bills	Make vacation reservations	Get a manicure
4:00 Tennis carpool			
5:00 _____	Make deposit		Buy a new journal
6:00 _____		Plan James's birthday party	
7:00 PTA meeting			Give myself a mud mask
8:00 _____			
9:00 _____			
10:00 _____			
11:00 _____			
MIDNIGHT _____			

NOTES

of our early summer family vacation, in which we snorkeled, swam, lived in bathing suits on the beach, and read books, was fading. I'd been busy getting James ready for camp, entertaining out-of-town guests, meeting so many work deadlines they were beginning to seem impossible. I needed a break. But there were four editors, three kids, two administrative assistants, and one spouse who all needed things from me—yesterday! I hadn't exactly been paying attention, and I was on the final countdown to meltdown.

It was time for emergency measures. So on a Sunday afternoon, Bill and I put leashes on our two Border collies, Kit and Sport, and headed to a nearby park that has miles of walking trails. During the course of the afternoon we talked in a way we hadn't had time to for a while. We traded information about the projects we're working on, which is always a shot in the arm for both of us. We're each other's best critics and cheerleaders. We talked about the kids. And we talked about ourselves as a couple. It wasn't a long retreat. It didn't involve a fancy, expensive candlelit dinner. It was only a couple of hours at the park, but it replenished both of us.

When we look optimistically for that hidden time, we find we can do five minutes of abdominal exercises or give ourselves a facial at home or read one chapter in a book on anger . . . and what do you know? We're making progress!

"If I had a dollar for every sock I've picked up, for every phone call I fielded, for every night I walked the floor with a sick baby, for every meal I cooked, for every time I cleaned the toilet . . ." I think we've all said this. It's an old saw, one I hear a little voice inside my head saying, even though I know being a family manager with all its mundane and not-so-mundane tasks is important. Most days I love both my jobs—as a family manager and as a writer and speaker. And for the most part, I'm a pretty darn good manager of time. I run a company, I manage a family of five (plus two dogs), and I actually have a life. But on the days when I find myself spending more time and energy than I plan for or can afford, I fantasize jumping on the next flight to anywhere. That's when I know it's time to be a caregiver—to myself.

Paying Attention

"I think the one lesson I have learned is there is no substitute for paying attention."
—Diane Sawyer

Attention is something everyone can afford to pay.

Mini-Choices Help Us Choose Wisely

How many choices and decisions do you figure each of us makes in a day? Ten? Twenty? A hundred? I think it's at least that many. And many of them are mini-choices. Excellence, as they say, is in the details—and it's in how we choose to spend our minutes, the mini-choices we make, that we change our lives.

Will I choose a cupcake or an apple? Will I drink a big glass of water or a glass of wine with dinner? Will I walk half a mile to the store with my youngest child or get in the car and drive there? Will I spend half an hour reading a book on starting a home-based business or will I call my best friend and complain about my job? Will I turn on the TV just to see what's on or play a game with my kids? Will I nag my husband about how we never spend any time together anymore, or will I tell him how much I miss him and invite him out for after-dinner coffee—even if it's only in the living room after the kids are in bed?

I can't even begin to think about how many mini-choices I make in any given day. What I do know is that once we begin to look at mini-choices—which often take only minutes—as ways to take care of ourselves, we've suddenly got time to do so.

An Invitation to a Treasure Hunt

TO: (Your Name Here)
FROM: (Your Name Here)
You are cordially invited to join me in a hunt for hidden treasure.
WHERE: Where you are now
WHEN: For a few minutes now and then, every day
Bring your thinking cap, your play clothes, your tired body and
 spirit. You won't regret it.

The Bottom Line

- Finding time to do what we want to do is as simple as one, two, three. One: Identify the time robbers in our lives. Two: Get rid of them. Three: Replace them with actions and activities that reflect the changes we want to make in our lives.
- Each and every one of us is robbed of something very valuable every day—our time—and it's taken from right under our own noses. The most common culprits are circumstances, daily activities, and ourselves.
- Each of us needs to make choices that protect and enhance our time for taking care of ourselves, doing what we need to do to nourish ourselves so we can be there for our families and the world at large.
- Every time you get interrupted it takes three minutes to get back on track.
- Never underestimate the potential of small snippets of time. Finding a nickel is not as exciting as finding a twenty-dollar bill, but you're still a nickel richer.
- There's no right or wrong way to spend a lunch hour. But sometimes it pays to think of alternative options.
- Knowing your priorities means knowing what you want to give time, emphasis, and care to in your life.
- Use a Daily Hit List to sort through and organize what you need to do each day.

FIVE

Building Equity
in You

"Invest in yourself." —William Feather

B uy low and sell high: what everyone who ever owned any stock wants to do! It's also what those of us who buy and sell houses try to do. Bill and I have been renovating houses for a number of years now. Buying a house with the intention of working on it to resell it at a higher price is a big risk and commitment. Not only that, but from experience I can tell you that it's more like working toward personal success than you might think.

First, a house is never done. By the time you get the kitchen redecorated, the bathrooms functioning, and the living room painted, you may need a new roof. Then it's time to paint the bedrooms and wallpaper the dining room, and lo and behold, the living room needs to be painted again. Then there's always ongoing maintenance—on the furnace, the appliances, the windows, the exterior.

Second, when you renovate a house you must make changes that add value to the house. Not every enhancement adds value, and some things you do to a house can lessen its value. (Installing a trickling waterfall in the master bedroom may remind you of your honeymoon in Maui, but it probably won't build up the

> "We create our fate every day we live."   —Henry Miller

equity in your house.) When Bill and I buy a house we try to be as careful as we can to make only the kinds of improvements that add value.

So it is with you and me—on both counts. First, we're never done. All of the things we want to change for the better in our lives are not going to happen today or tomorrow. And even after a lot of the changes have been made, there will always be something else we need to work on. We will always be a project in progress, hopefully getting better and better.

Second, what we do to ourselves, the choices we make every hour of every day, can add value to our self-worth and help us achieve personal success.

Taking Stock

When Bill and I redo a house, we begin by taking stock: evaluating what changes need to be made and what resources we have to work with. Then we envision what the house will look like after we've made the changes. I've found that this evaluation-and-envisioning process is actually a good model to use on myself.

About once a year, I give myself the gift of taking stock. I take myself and my notepad off to a quiet spot where I can have an honest chat with myself. I methodically go through each area of my life, making notes on my physical, mental, emotional, and spiritual states—sort of my own private job review for the Personal Management part of my family manager job. I check myself over from head to

> "You never find yourself until you face the truth."
> —Pearl Bailey

toe—my shape and appear-
ance, my emotional state. I
examine what I've learned
(and where I need to learn
more) and my spiritual life.

> "There isn't a person anywhere who isn't capable of doing more than he thinks he can."
> —Henry Ford

I take a good, hard look at things as they are. The first question
is, What do I look like now?

The second question is, What do I want to look like? My focus
is on areas I want to enhance or need to grow in. I usually end up
with fairly eclectic lists of what I need and want for myself in the
physical, mental, emotional, and spiritual categories of my personal life.

It's almost as if I have three mirrors: the one in which I see myself as I look now; the one in which I see myself as I'll look in the
short-term future; and the one in which I see myself as I'll look
when I achieve a long-held dream. Say, for example, you want to lose
twenty-five pounds. You'd start with a good, long look in the mirror
of the here and now. In fact, looking in that mirror is probably what
moved you to want to lose the weight! In the mirror for the short-
term future, you might see yourself tomorrow morning, getting up
twenty minutes earlier than usual to take a brisk walk. Then you
might see yourself eating carrot sticks instead of corn chips at
lunchtime. In the mirror for the long-term, you'll see a more slen-
der, energetic you—with a new look and new exercise and eating
habits.

Important note: As I as-
sess myself and look for
areas in which I need im-
provement, I am kind to myself. No one benefits from
harsh criticism.

> "Women are their own worst enemies. And guilt is the main weapon of self-torture."
> —Erica Jong

> "Progress is looking forward intelligently, looking within critically, and moving on incessantly."
> —Waldo Pondray Warren

Evaluate, then Envision

We owe ourselves an honest, rigorous evaluation of both our strong and our weak points. I know many women who don't realize they're letting themselves go. One woman I know doesn't have a full-length mirror in her house because she doesn't want to see the whole picture. That's not healthy or helpful.

On the other hand, we need to look at the positives, too. Perhaps you completed only one class toward a nursing degree. That's one more than none! We need to give ourselves credit. We need to remember that we can't do everything at once.

Bring Your Assets into Focus

Consider the following categories when reminding yourself of your assets:

Personal Strengths. What are you good at? What do you love to do?

Learned Skills. What skills and wisdom have you gained over the course of your life?

Education. What skills and knowledge have you acquired formally?

Experiences. What perspectives, insights, or knowledge have you picked up along the way?

Family, Friends, and Their Network. You are probably only one or two persons away from knowing someone who has what you need or knows what you need to know.

Access to Authority and Expertise. Who do you know that can open doors for you and give you the information you need?

Special Environmental Opportunities. What freedoms and resources do you have available to you in your city, state, or country?

Physical Abilities and Attributes. What physical traits do you have going for you?

Financial Resources. What financial assets do you have access to?

Also examine the areas you are dissatisfied with. Dissatisfaction in itself isn't harmful unless you take out your frustration on others or let it lead you to despair. It's the burr under the saddle, the nagging feeling that compels you to action. If you want something really badly, you may be driven to find a way to get to it.

Sifting for Specifics

Think about how you can make your dream happen. Imagine yourself in your dream situation. For example, envision a dream job. Ask yourself, What does the office look like? What tasks would I spend the most time on? How much time would I spend working alone and with others? What kind of people would I like to work with? What skills do I have that would make me successful at this venture? What experience do I bring to the table? Are there companies near me where this

> "Restlessness and discontent are the necessities of progress."
> —Thomas Alva Edison

position might exist? Do I have contacts with people in any of those companies?

The first time I did this evaluation/envision exercise I was thirty-five years old and had three children, ages eleven, seven, and six months. When I looked in the mirror I saw a woman desperate for adult company. I felt trapped in a wilderness of diapers, action figures, and Richard Scarry books, a woman whose emotions were so out of whack that Harrison Ford could have walked through the door and I would have snapped his head off.

I was sluggish from lack of exercise and not sleeping well. My hairdo was dated and unmanageable. I felt spiritually dry; I had little inner strength to meet the tasks of the day, let alone meet them with serenity and optimism.

In other words, the woman I saw was not the woman I'd planned to be. This state of being didn't happen overnight. As Benjamin Franklin said, "A little neglect may breed great mischief. . . . For want of a nail the shoe was lost; for want of a shoe the horse was lost; for want of a horse the rider was lost." I would add, for want of paying attention to myself, I now had a mountain of work to do to restore the vision I once had for myself.

Sample Evaluation/Envision Exercise

Here's what a sample review might look like. It's both taking stock of what is and looking at what could be.

PHYSICAL ASSESSMENT
What do I look like now? What do I want to look like? What could be better? How could I be healthier? More balanced? More attractive?

- Schedule a physical exam. (Short-term: Do this ASAP.)
- Go through wardrobe and give away clothes I don't wear anymore. (Short-term.)
- Buy new clothes. (Long-term. See below.)
- Talk with my hairdresser about an easier, updated style. (Short-term.)
- My arms seem to be getting shorter. Schedule an eye exam. (Short-term. ASAP.)
- I've been feeling run-down lately. Get more exercise and sleep. (Short-term: Add a ten-minute walk to my day. Long-term: Build up to a more rigorous exercise program. Join a gym. After six months, reevaluate sleep needs in light of exercise.)
- Look into weight-loss programs. (Wait until I lose weight to buy clothes? Research options ASAP.)
- Reorganize my closet and drawers. (Long-term: Look into having a consultant come in to help me. Price closet organizers.)
- Think I'd feel better about getting into shape if I had a few new outfits that fit me now and look good. (Budget for this over the next three months.)
- My fingernails need help. (Schedule and budget for monthly manicures.)
- Look into new cosmetics product line. (Want something that's simple to use, but will soften my skin.)

_____

_____

_____

_____

_____

_____

_____

_____

_____

_____

_____

_____

_____

_____

_____

_____

_____

_____

_____

EMOTIONAL ASSESSMENT

What do I feel like now? What do I want to feel like? What could be better? How could I be emotionally healthier?

- Work on my attitude. (Short-term: ASAP. Remind myself what I have to be grateful for.)
- Get more exercise and sleep. (See previous.)
- Spend more time with my spouse. (Talk with him about a weekly date.)
- Find quotes that remind me that when life hands me lemons I can make lemonade or a soufflé. Post them where I'll see them.
- Schedule fun time for myself. (Short-term: Call a friend and ask her out for lunch. Long-term: Look ahead at my calendar and make sure I'm scheduling fun activities as well as work-related things.)
- Begin to deal with ongoing problems; don't assume they'll go away by themselves, and don't try to bury feelings of sadness or frustration. (Short-term: Make some notes about my emotional life and how I'd like it to change. Long-term: Explore whether I might want to enlist the help of a professional counselor.)
- Have a plan for blah days. (Short-term: Make a list of pick-me-ups I can pull off in a pinch, like taking in a matinee, getting a massage, walking around a museum or park one afternoon while a sitter watches the kids.)

MENTAL ASSESSMENT

How knowledgeable am I now? How knowledgeable do I want to be? How could I make myself more interesting?

- Start a list of books I want to read this year. (Renew library card. Budget for books I want to buy.)
- Look into a computer class. (Call college. Call computer manufacturers to see what they recommend.)
- Make a folder for clippings from newspapers and magazines that will help me be more up-to-date at work. (Try this. See if it helps.)
- Make a work space for reading and writing at home. (Look into a new desk, desk lamp, chair. Budget. Maybe check garage sales.)
- Begin a list of vocabulary words for the refrigerator. (Right away. Invite the kids to add to it, too.)
- Start a book group. (Long-term: Get a group going. Short-term: Invite two friends to read a book and meet to discuss it.)
- Sign up for lecture series. (Check different options at library and college. Invite my husband or a friend to join me?)

SPIRITUAL ASSESSMENT

How well do I react to daily ups and downs? How could I be healthier? More balanced? More serene?

- Set aside quiet time for prayer every day. (Begin now. Continue. Write it in my schedule.)
- Take a class at church. (Long-term: Look into fall offerings.)
- Make a list of books in this field I want to read. (Combine with previous book list.)
- Take a bigger chunk of time out to grow spiritually. (Long-term: Look into going away on a spiritual retreat.)
- Share my spiritual life with others. (Ongoing. Schedule time with my spouse and/or friends to talk about concerns we have for our own spiritual lives and those of our children. Maybe take a retreat together. See above.)
- Remind myself that God provides. (Short-term: Find inspirational quotes so that I remember that this is true. Write them out and place them where I'll see them frequently.)
- Seek out a spiritual mentor. (Pastor? Wise friend? Find someone who can recommend books to read and talk with me.)

_____

_____

_____

_____

_____

_____

_____

_____

_____

_____

_____

_____

_____

_____

_____

_____

_____

_____

IMAGINE IMPROVEMENT

Looking into the mirror of our future means envisioning what isn't yet, based on what is. In short, I'm never

> "Imagination is more important than knowledge."
> —Albert Einstein

going to be a nuclear physicist. My talents and experience lie in other areas. But that doesn't mean I'm not going to continue trying to learn new things for the rest of my life.

What I'm really doing is building a vision, *a clear mental image of a future preferable to my current state.* (Remember that the future is the next hour just as much as it is the next year.) This vision should be describable, not inchoate. Take some time to paint this picture for yourself. It can be general at first. Maybe it's your dream job. What would suit you? Or you'd like to learn a new skill. Maybe you'd like to start a support group of some kind, become an expert cook, volunteer for a specific charity, or learn to play golf.

If you're having trouble painting even a general picture, try the following exercises. You don't need to limit yourself to three answers for each question. But I've found that the first three things that come immediately to your mind often are your heart's secret desires.

- Write down three things you used to enjoy doing and would like to do again. Sewing? Working math equations? Helping children learn to read? Taking a class? Jogging? Cooking?
- Write down three things you would like to try at

> "The future belongs to those who believe in the beauty of their dreams."
> —Eleanor Roosevelt
>
> Look at one area in your life that you have tried to change in the past but haven't. What is the payoff for still being where you are? Take one step today to make a change.

least once to see if you like them. Volunteering at a food bank? Wind-surfing? Writing and submitting an article to your local newspaper?

- Write down three things you'd like to change about your appearance.
- Write down three habits you'd like to lose.
- Write down three habits you'd like to incorporate into your life.
- Write down three hobbies that sound fun.
- Write down three skills you would like to learn.
- Find a bulletin for a local community college. Write down three classes that sound interesting.
- Look at the want ads in the newspaper, and note three jobs that sound interesting.

Once you've done all this, go back over your list. Who is the person who would like to do these things? How does she spend her time? What does she look like? Would you like to know her better? Are you beginning to see her?

The more practice we have at making mental pictures, the easier visualizing gets.

Future Tense

Future, as I've said, refers to our ability to focus our sights on the horizon two days from now, a month from now, a year from now. The wonderful thing about envisioning the future is that when we do so, we're giving ourselves permission to say: This is how I want to look, how I want to live, what I want to do then. We're allowing ourselves to dream. When we concentrate on the future, instead

> "All the resources we need are in the mind."
> —Theodore Roosevelt, Jr.

of on the past, we're less likely to beat up on ourselves for not being, doing, looking like we want to in the future. We can let the past be the past and look toward the days ahead.

Of course, once we've envisioned any possible future action, we have to decide if it's something we want to carry out or just to keep in mind to look at again later. You might explore some visions of the future and then decide to give them up entirely. For instance, a divorced friend of mine whose children are grown decided that she'd be happier if she moved to a smaller town in the Midwest rather than continuing to live in a large city on the West Coast. But after envisioning herself there—where she'd live, what she'd do—she decided that she really had too strong a support group and too good (albeit not perfect) a situation to move. Instead she focused her attention on making other changes in her life.

Desirable is the other key word in envisioning. I'm not asking you to envision what you *should* do or be, by your own or anybody else's standards. Your vision of the future should involve what *you* feel is pleasing, advantageous, improvement-oriented, and worth seeking.

THE LONG-TERM MIRROR

Another way to work with visions is to see yourself in the far-off future. What are the most wonderful things that could happen to you during the rest of your life? If you could accomplish anything, what would it be? What rewards would you be enjoying as a result of your accomplishment?

In my own case I saw myself pursuing a career in writing and speaking, getting into my size 8 pants, becoming self-disciplined, growing

> "There is nothing like a dream to create the future."
> —Victor Hugo

more gracious, drawing on inner strength I gathered daily through inspirational reading and prayer. I desired a new level of physical fitness, intellectual astuteness, professional fulfillment, spiritual centeredness, and emotional balance. Reaching such a place would not only bring order to my personal chaos but would make me rich in resources for those I loved.

It's important to know that visions may change midstream. In one of the houses Bill and I renovated, I had a very firm vision of what the kitchen would eventually look like. As things turned out, even though we had estimated the cost in time and money as well as the potential added value of new cabinets, we couldn't put them in. The costs were way out of line relative to the added value. We decided that our desire to resell the house at a profit was still the top priority. So we did not implement that particular part of the vision and lived with the cupboards as they were until we sold the house.

As you envision your future self, you'll need to be flexible as well as focused.

Vision: Why It's Worth Having

A vision is . . .
- central to your success in living out your personal best
- inspiring, energizing
- change-oriented
- challenging
- unique: custom-fitted to you

A vision gives you . . .
- a purpose beyond surviving the day
- a sense of continuity, a bridge to the next goal, a reason to go on
- direction to see where you are in relation to where you want to be

- heart to face the future with anticipation rather than with fear and uncertainty

A vision increases your interest, commitment, and productivity. You're able to explain why you want change and know you're working to shape your future. It gives you a ruler to measure satisfaction against: you know when you're making progress. A vision makes it possible to make better decisions because you know exactly what you want in the end.

Fuel for Action

A vision is fuel for action, for only by acting can we test our vision—see if it's one we want to pursue. Beginning to act on a vision can lead us to all sorts of wonderful new places. So visualize yourself taking steps.

Remember, this is an in-process vision. It's neither the you of now nor the you who will have a new job or a new look, whatever you envisioned to begin with. Be patient with yourself. Visions take time to come to fruition. Be aware of what resources you have at hand, and picture yourself using them.

If you were highly motivated, would you be on the Internet searching for information about menopause remedies? Would you be putting your résumé together? Would you be picking up the phone to research adult education classes you might take?

Some people are good at envisioning what they want their future to hold. I have one friend who's good at writing scenarios. She has an abundance of good ideas of how life could be, too many to fit into her life, so she's started

> "We are either progressing or retrograding all the while; there is no such thing as remaining stationary in life."
> —James Freeman Clarke

> "The way to get ahead is to start now. If you start now, you will know a lot next year that you don't know now and that you would not have known next year if you had waited."
> —William Feather

writing fiction. This same friend is pretty good at knowing her own shortcomings, and she maintains that it's not envisioning a different self that's difficult—it's figuring out how to get herself there.

When it comes to envisioning scenarios, family managers generally fit into one of two camps. There's Camp Plethora, in which women see so many choices they have difficulty identifying their priorities and getting on with the process of making changes. Then there's Camp Scarcity, in which women feel that they have no options at all. Neither of these camps is a very comfortable place to be.

And the road out of them is the same: start small, and don't sell yourself short.

If I live in Camp Plethora, I may envision myself going to graduate school, working at my ideal job, volunteering time for a worthy cause I believe in, living in a house that better suits my family's needs, entertaining at elegant dinner parties, being twenty-five pounds lighter, and feeling happier. The problem is I don't know where to start. I want to live in a different house, so I do nothing to enhance the one I now live in. Because I also want to go to school and change jobs, I don't do the research and groundwork that might eventually lead my family to a new house. In the meantime, I'm not losing weight because I don't have time to exercise because, because, because . . . But if I start small—say, by beginning to exercise twenty minutes a day—things begin to change. I lose weight. I have more energy. And a bit at a time, my visions seem like they might happen.

If I live in Camp Scarcity, I may know only that I don't like things the way they are. I don't know what might make me happier. I can't see myself in a different job or a different house. And maybe, indeed, I don't want to change those areas. But I'm tired and cranky all the time. If I start small—again, by beginning to exercise twenty minutes a day—I have more energy. With that energy comes the ability to see that, for example, my job is not using my best talents, and that's making me cranky and tired. So I start to think about changing jobs.

A Checklist for Your Chosen Actions

Whichever camp we find ourselves in at a particular time, it's good to have a reality check. These are questions that I use to help myself clarify if and how I'm going to put a vision into action. They're good to ask ourselves when we're implementing a new vision and hit a rough patch.

• *Can I really do it?* It's probably not realistic for a family manager with an outside career and three small children to go on an archaeological dig to pursue her interest in ancient civilizations. It might, on the other hand, be realistic to read new books on archaeology, to take a class, or to participate in a hands-on project at the science museum with her eight-year-old. Let me emphasize, though, that no two mothers are alike. Doable means doable for you—not your mother, your best friend, or anybody else.

• *Am I thinking in terms of concrete, manageable tasks?* "Get in shape" is not an action plan. It might be the vision, but it's not the how-to. The actions you take might be: walk twenty minutes five times a week; join a gym and take a strength-building class; go cycling with your ten-year-old twice a week.

• *Am I thinking of myself as a good girl when I follow through with my intended actions, and a bad girl when I don't?* Following a plan is neither a carrot nor a stick. Admitting to ourselves when we didn't do what we set out to do and setting a corrective course is a good idea; beating ourselves up because we didn't check off every item on our action plan is not. Rewarding ourselves for a job well done, especially with something nurturing and good for us— maybe a massage or half an hour in a scented bath with the telephone turned off and the door locked—is not a bad idea. But then again, we might need that bath or that massage more when we're feeling down because we haven't been doing the tasks we set for ourselves.

• *Am I taking into account the reality that our visions change and so do the ways we choose to implement them?* Once you've written a list of the things you're going to do toward implementing your vision, don't throw away the pen. Take that shaping-up example again. You've begun walking twenty minutes a day. You look into gyms near you, and in the process you come across an ad for dance classes. You remember how much you loved dancing as a teen, so you abandon the gym research and enroll in a dance class. Are you abandoning your chosen path? I don't think so.

Action breeds action. Don't be surprised if you find that as you accomplish the items on your list, you have renewed energy and enthusiasm. Once we start to develop healthful habits, new ways of caring for ourselves often occur to us. All of a sudden we realize that we do indeed see ourselves with new eyes, we have a new vision of who we are, and we're on the road to becoming our personal best.

Remember: Buy low, sell high. Start to value yourself in small ways and watch your value grow. Start to make

> "Growth itself contains the germ of happiness."
> —Pearl Buck

small changes in your life, and watch yourself move toward personal success.

The Bottom Line

- As I look for areas in which I need improvement, I am kind to myself, for no one benefits from harsh criticism.
- Identifying areas ripe for change in your life is not about whining, finding fault, or listing excuses for why you can't initiate change.
- Making an honest, objective evaluation is about acknowledging that you have untapped potential and making plans to tap it.
- When you envision the future, you're giving yourself permission to say: This is how I want to look, how I want to live, what I want to do then. You're allowing yourself to dream.
- Know that a vision may change midstream.
- "Think of what you can do with what there is." —Ernest Hemingway
- Don't sell yourself short!

SIX

A Healthier,
More Attractive You

"Health is the thing that makes you feel that now is the best
time of the year."   —Franklin P. Adams

In our culture, health and beauty are not necessarily related.
And we tend to put the emphasis, especially for women, on the
latter. Health, although certainly a concern, runs a distant second and is often defined in ways that get confused with beauty—
thin, young, trim, fit. "In shape" is rarely measured relative to age,
gender, body type, and lifestyle. It seems to mean qualifying for
the swimsuit issue of a sports magazine.

Let's face it: very few of us are natural waifs, nor should we
aspire to be. We take a giant step toward taking control of our
lives in a way that promotes a healthful self-image and wise self-
management when we give up this delusion. If I exercise regularly
but still have less-than-chic thighs, am I inferior? I don't think so.
Wise self-management of our bodies isn't just about looking great
or even making the most of the equipment we've been given. It's
about caring for our one and only body in a way that promotes and
increases health, energy, and longevity—three things we can all
make good use of.

There's nothing wrong with wanting to look attractive. I want to be suitable for business, presentable for company, and comfortable for everything. I also want my family

> "The first wealth is health."
> —Ralph Waldo Emerson

to be proud of me. I want to be my best for myself, too. I know that when I feel good about how I look and feel, I'm free to love and give myself to others. The more confident I am, the more I accomplish.

But there's more to it than that. Looking our best often means feeling our best. It means having both the energy and the self-esteem necessary to reach out and achieve our dreams, to become personally successful.

Wise self-management of our bodies also builds stamina. We can more easily go with less sleep for brief periods. Our bodies bounce back from minor illnesses more quickly. We feel better about ourselves and can live with setbacks in our careers or our personal lives more easily.

Wise self-management of our bodies involves practice in three areas: food, exercise, and appearance. They're separate but interrelated. As you read through the chapter, choose the ideas and practices that appeal to you. Give yourself permission to try new things.

About Food

Weight loss is a $4 billion-a-year business. According to a report from the Centers for Disease Control and Prevention, on any given day half of American women are dieting. For years I could count myself among these women. I think I tried almost every diet known to humankind, from the cabbage-soup diet (which was just as bad as it sounds) to the low-carbohydrate-eat-all-the-protein-and-fat-you-want diet, which didn't work for me *at all*. All the protein I wanted—my breakfast consisted of three extra-large eggs scrambled in butter and smothered with cheese, with sausage and bacon on the side—added up to about 5,000 calories a day. I gained five pounds the first week.

It wasn't until I learned that the only diet that works is the one I can stick with for the rest of my life that I truly took control of this area. Look carefully at the word *die-t*. That should tell us something. When we diet our body's ability to burn calories actually dies. Understanding these facts made a huge difference in my health and appearance. It can in yours, too. Here's why.

First, when you go on a diet, instead of losing fat cells, you encourage the loss of muscle cells that burn fat. Think of your body as one of those gas-guzzling cars from the sixties. They had big engines that burned a lot of fuel. Your muscles are the engine that burns the fuel (calories) you put into your body. Many dieters think they're losing fat when they reduce their caloric intake, but unfortunately, muscle cells—the body's engine—are also lost. Exercise combined with a low-calorie diet can help reduce the loss of muscle tissue, but our bodies still use some muscle tissue to meet energy demands when there aren't enough calories.

Second, when you diet, you rob your body of the energy it needs to burn fat correctly—through more physical activity. Really, how much get-up-and-go can you muster to get yourself to the gym if you subsist on green vegetables and rice cakes? As strange as it seems, if we want to burn fat we have to take in enough quality calories to give our bodies the energy to do fat-burning exercise.

Third, dieting lowers the rate at which your body burns calories. If you feed your body 500 calories a day, it automatically goes into starvation mode. It thinks it's dying, and it wants to survive! To do so, it slows down and burns calories at a much slower rate.

On the other hand, exercise does exactly the opposite. It sets into motion biochemical changes that speed up calorie-burning.

So let's make a deal: no more diets. From now on it's *lifestyle*. This is part of taking control of your life: changing the way you eat in healthful, positive ways so that you feel and look your best for the rest of your life.

How Many Calories Do You Need?

Taking control of your life by practicing healthful eating habits begins with knowing your body. To know approximately how many calories a day you need to maintain your weight, find your CQ—calorie quotient.

- If you're practically sedentary or exercise only occasionally, multiply your weight by 12.
- If you're moderately active (a half hour of steady aerobic work, three to six times a week), multiply by 15.
- If you're a committed exerciser (an hour or more a day of vigorous activity), multiply by 18.

The best way to lose weight is to lower your CQ and to exercise. Since a pound of fat contains approximately 3,500 calories, if you lower your daily caloric intake by 500, for example, you will lose a pound a week. When I first heard that fact I felt discouraged, because I wanted to lose more than a pound a week. Then on a trip to the grocery store I found a one-pound package of ground beef and visualized that much "meat" coming off of my backside. Then I pictured another one-pound package coming off of my thighs. To this day, when I put on a little weight over the holidays or on a vacation, I stand in front of a full-length mirror and do my "meat routine." This helps me take the weight off again, slowly but surely.

Diet, Schmiet

- Make a list of all the times you've tried to diet. Add to the list the negative effects those attempts had on your life.
- Make another list of positive changes you would like to see in your life. How does your weight affect those changes?
- Starting today: (1) Disengage yourself from conversations concerning dieting and eating. (2) Never again buy clothes that are too small in the hopes that you will one day fit into them. You're setting yourself up for failure and a constant reminder that you aren't where you want to be.

HEALTHFUL EATING HABITS

- Stock your pantry and refrigerator with healthful foods that are ready to eat or quickly and easily prepared.
- Avoid refined sugar and high-carbohydrate foods, since this leads to the storage of excess fat in your body.
- Don't buy foods that tempt you. If you know you can't eat just one, leave them at the store!
- Drink a lot of water. Determine how much water you need each day by dividing your weight in two. This gives you the total number of ounces. Divide that amount by 8 to determine how many glasses. So, for example, if you weigh 140 pounds, you should drink 70 ounces of water a day. Seventy divided by 8 equals 8.75. So you should be drinking about nine 8-ounce glasses of water a day.
- Bake, broil, or roast instead of frying.
- Allow yourself only three taste samples of whatever you're cooking.
- Take at least one multivitamin and mineral supplement daily.

- Maintain a weekly menu plan and count your calories for each meal.
- Never shop for groceries on an empty stomach. You'll be more likely to yield to tempting displays.
- Become familiar with food labels and learn to buy only what is good for you.
- Eat when you are hungry. Stop when you are full.
- Brush your teeth after every meal. You'll be less inclined to continue nibbling.
- Never eat standing up.
- Put less food on your fork or spoon, and take smaller bites.
- Wait ten minutes before snacking. The urge might pass.
- Even if you eat alone, don't watch TV or read while you eat. While I'm usually all in favor of multitasking, eating is not exactly a task. We tend to pay too little attention to what we eat anyway. It's too easy to keep eating long after we're full if we're engrossed in a book or a TV program.
- Be an early-bird eater. Your body burns calories most efficiently during the first twelve hours of the day. So eat at least 25 percent of your calories at breakfast and the same at lunch. Don't eat anything after eight o'clock in the evening.
- Eat slowly and play calm background music while you eat. Research shows we eat faster when we listen to fast music while eating.
- Imagine yourself thinner. This will keep you going.
- Say this aloud to yourself five times a day: "I take good care of myself. I eat wisely, and I am growing healthier and trimmer every day."
- Don't assume healthful eating means torturing yourself with foods you dislike day after day. Instead, find good-food choices you enjoy.

> "After thirty, the body has a mind of its own."
> —Bette Midler

- Allow yourself 200 to 300 calories' worth of favorite foods each day.
- On days you know you'll be eating treats—a slice of birthday cake, a holiday meal, party hors d'oeuvres—cut back on your overall calorie intake so you won't compromise your goals.
- Pack your own snacks when you're traveling.
- Read books on health and nutrition.

Think About This

A friend of mine told me she met a man at her weight-loss group who'd just had knee surgery. His doctor told him that for every pound he lost he was taking seventeen pounds of pressure off his knees. Wow!

HOW TO CUT BACK ON FAT

- Become an avid label reader.
- Allow soups and stews to chill after cooking so you can see the fat and skim it off.
- Switch to low- and nonfat dairy products. Many taste as good as high-fat products.
- Use fat-burning spices. A British study showed that adding hot chili sauce and spicy yellow mustard to a meal increased study subjects' metabolism up to 25 percent for the next three hours. A mere three-fifths of a teaspoon can do the trick.
- Substitute applesauce for oil in baked products. (Applesauce contains pectin, which helps maintain a moist texture. How-

ever, if the recipe's only liquid is oil, you may need to use half applesauce and half nonfat milk to ensure moistness.)

- Use cholesterol-free egg substitutes or egg whites instead of whole eggs in any recipe. (Substitute two egg whites for one whole egg.)
- Substitute nonfat plain yogurt for sour cream when baking. Or place one sixteen-ounce carton of nonfat cottage cheese in a blender with two tablespoons of nonfat yogurt and two tablespoons of lemon juice. Blend until smooth and use instead of sour cream.
- When sautéing, use wine, nonfat cooking spray, or chicken broth instead of oil.
- Emphasize natural flavors in products. Experiment with spices and fruit juices to add that extra punch to your recipes.
- Invest in a good low-fat cookbook with easy-to-fix recipes.

Did You Know . . . ?

Your body has 60,000 miles of blood vessels. If you are 25 pounds overweight, your heart must pump blood through an extra 5,000 miles of blood vessels.

TIPS FOR EATING OUT

Eating out can be a painful experience when you're trying to eat wisely and/or lose weight. Everyone around you orders that high-fat appetizer and cheers when the dessert tray arrives. Choose your meal carefully and without self-pity. You're on a worthy path to health, and you can still enjoy a meal you don't have to cook. Savvy ordering is the key to eating out without pigging out. Here are some tips.

Appetizers

- Skip the cocktail or limit yourself to one wine spritzer. Alcohol cuts willpower and whets the appetite. Choose iced tea or water with a slice of lime or lemon.
- Have fish, raw vegetables, or fruit. Avoid rich sauces, dips, and batter-fried anything.
- Eat a few small bites of bread without butter or margarine.

Entrees

- Ask for a half portion. It's well worth it, even if you have to pay full price.
- Choose an appetizer, with or without a salad, as a main dish.
- Look for terms such as *steamed, broiled, grilled, roasted, poached,* or *simmered* as indicators of a more healthful meal.
- Don't choose foods that are buttered, fried, creamed, scalloped, rich; come with gravy or cheese sauce; or are served au gratin, in a pastry, or cooked in oil.
- Order a low-fat fish such as cod, halibut, sole, snapper, swordfish, or shark.
- Stop eating when you are full.

Vegetables and Salads

- Avoid high-fat dressings, bacon, egg, and cheese at the salad bar.
- Use vinegar, vinegar and oil, lemon juice, or diet dressing as your salad dressing.
- Look for vegetables seasoned with lemon or herbs rather than fat and salt.
- Ask for a baked potato (without the butter) instead of fries or chips.

Desserts

- Look for fruit on the dessert menu. If you don't see it, ask your server if you could order a small plate of fruit.
- Order a light, low-fat dessert such as sherbet, sorbet, or angel food cake.
- If you decide on a richer dessert, share it with someone else.
- Have a cup of coffee, tea, or cappuccino made with skim milk. If you have a hankering for something sweet, a teaspoon of sugar in coffee has many fewer calories than a piece of chocolate cake.

Food Fact

Restaurant portions are geared to men's appetites, which means they contain a third to a half more food than the average woman needs to maintain her weight.

SEEK SUPPORT

Consider joining a weight-loss program or going to a self-help support group. It's easier to maintain changes in our lives when we have support. Check the yellow pages for a program near you. Churches, neighborhood centers, Ys, and other community-based organizations often offer such support groups.

LIFESTYLE: FOUR STEPS TO BETTER FOCUS

1. Stop dieting. It makes you focus on yourself, your body, and food. Therefore, dieting provides the perfect arena for you to grow to love food more and love yourself less.
2. Don't focus on what other people think. No one's calling your character into question when you eat a piece of pecan pie or canonizing you for skipping dessert.

3. Stop feeling like a failure. You haven't been able to lose weight and overcome the power of food because you've been using the wrong methods. Try a new perspective and allow it to give you hope.

4. Know your enemy. Understand that what you are attacking is the behavior of overindulgence: the food does not need to change, your actions do.

About Exercise

Think tortoise and hare. For beginning exercisers, this is especially important. Slow and steady wins the race, the day, the personal best for each of us. Even those among us who exercise regularly would do well to remember this maxim. Yes, it's good to push ourselves, to build up our stamina and endurance over time. But doing too much too fast eventually earns us the hare's booby prize—or a pulled tendon, a strained muscle, a bad back. (Not to mention the discouragement that follows.)

You wouldn't ask a baby to solve a calculus problem. You probably wouldn't ask a grandmother to name today's top ten tunes on the pop chart. So why do we ask ourselves to try to exercise in ways that are inappropriate—and probably dangerous—for our age and physical condition? The best way to start is by knowing your body.

Normal bodily processes such as breathing and the digestion of food burn calories to provide you with energy. The rate at which you burn calories while at rest is called your resting metabolic rate. A person with a slow metabolism burns fewer calories at rest than a person with a fast metabolic rate. Some overweight people have a slower metabolic rate than people of normal weight, giving them a tendency to gain weight. Metabolic rate appears to be inherited, but we can increase our rate with exercise. Muscle burns more calories than fat.

If you haven't been involved in an exercise program for a long time, particularly if you're over forty or overweight, consult your doctor before beginning. Remember, exercise doesn't have to be expensive or fancy. You don't need a large wardrobe, state-of-the-art equipment, or a membership in an exclusive gym.

Try to exercise aerobically at least three hours each week. Join an aerobic dance class, swim laps, ride a bicycle, jog, jump rope, or walk briskly during your lunch break. If you can't join a class, try jogging in place every morning while you watch the news.

THIRTY-ONE EXERCISE FAVORS
YOU CAN DO YOURSELF

1. Don't look for the closest parking place.
2. Do your own yard work.
3. Play active games with your kids: hopscotch, basketball, jump rope.
4. Take a walk with a friend instead of sitting together to talk.
5. Ride your bike to the store or work.
6. Take a walk with your child in a baby carrier or a stroller.
7. On weekends, schedule time for active family fun—take a bike ride, go on a hike, play tennis, or swim.
8. Walk up a few flights of stairs to an appointment instead of getting on the elevator.
9. Do deep knee bends while drying your hair.
10. Do sit-ups and other floor exercises while watching TV.
11. Pack and unload your own groceries.
12. Hang laundry out on the clothesline to dry.
13. Do isometric exercises while you drive. Tighten your tummy, buttocks, and thighs.
14. While you're on the phone, pick up a pair of three-pound weights and work your biceps.
15. Go bowling as a family.

16. Mix cake batter by hand instead of using a mixer.

17. Wash your own car.

18. Do calf raises while you work at the kitchen counter.

19. If you're delayed, make the most of it. Go for a brisk walk in the airport terminal while waiting for a flight. Walk around the block while waiting for a table in a restaurant. Tell your doctor's receptionist that you'll be walking in the hall until they're ready for you.

20. Carry your own luggage to and from cars, to airport check-ins, to your hotel room.

21. Walk to lunch instead of getting in your car.

22. Help friends move boxes into their new apartment or house.

23. Take your kids to a roller-skating rink and get out there with them.

24. Swing your arms while you walk.

25. Keep an exercise mat easily accessible and do leg lifts while dinner is cooking.

26. I wear five-pound weights on each ankle when puttering around the house. Walking to the laundry room and back, from the kitchen to the office, becomes a mini-workout.

27. Be alert for unusual times to exercise. Squeeze your fanny muscles when you're riding in an elevator, waiting in a long line, or caught in a traffic jam. When you do housework, bend, stretch, and move briskly.

> Walking is the easiest exercise to start. It strengthens your body and relaxes your mind. It requires no expensive equipment (only a good pair of walking shoes), no training, and no expensive facilities.

28. Do fifty crunches before bed.

29. Get up half an hour earlier and go for a walk before jumping in the shower.

30. Walk whenever you can—down to your mailbox, to the store.

31. Weight should not affect whether or not you go swimming, dancing, in-line skating, out to eat, anything. Go now, not ten pounds from now.

TWENTY-ONE REASONS TO EXERCISE

Regular exercise:

1. Builds strong muscles and bones
2. Strengthens your heart
3. Reduces your risk of chronic diseases, including heart disease, osteoporosis, and high blood pressure
4. Helps control your weight
5. Reduces your risk of many types of cancer
6. Slows the aging process
7. Reduces symptoms of PMS
8. Relieves menstrual pain
9. Improves your self-image
10. Relieves depression
11. Improves the quality of your sleep
12. Improves your posture
13. Improves the quality of your life, particularly as you age
14. Increases your metabolism and decreases your appetite
15. Releases stress
16. Reduces the severity of varicose veins
17. Gives you more energy
18. Increases your resistance to fatigue
19. Helps you to be more productive at work
20. Builds stamina for other physical activities
21. Increases your feeling of well-being

Did You Know?

Researchers at the University of Vermont in Burlington recently found that a flagging metabolism is not an inevitable part of aging. It's due primarily to a loss of muscle mass. After the mid-twenties, an average adult loses half a pound of muscle every year. According to Dr. Ken Cooper in his book *Regaining the Power of Youth at Any Age*, until the age of fifty you lose 4 percent of strength and muscle mass per decade. After that, the loss increases to about 10 percent per decade.

PUT MUSCLE INTO YOUR DAY

The best way to add muscle mass is through weight training. You can use health-club weight machines, take a weight-training class, or work out at home with a set of free weights, about 3 to 5 pounds each. Besides the general benefits we just listed, weight training and other exercise can increase your resting metabolic rate by as much as 5 to 10 percent for several hours afterward, sparking what is known as the afterburn effect. After two months you'll add enough muscle to burn about 108 additional calories each day. For specific exercises, consult a fitness professional or another reliable source.

Formula for Fitness

To avoid the loss of muscle mass that accompanies age, Dr. Ken Cooper suggests using the following formula in balancing aerobic and strength training (weight lifting):

Age 40 and under	80% aerobic, 20% strength training
Age 41–50	70% aerobic, 30% strength training
Age 51–60	60% aerobic, 40% strength training
Age 61 and up	55% aerobic, 45% strength training

DON'T LET THAT AEROBICS CLASS INTIMIDATE YOU

If you usually slink by the aerobics room because aerobics make you feel like a klutz, you're missing a fun alternative for cardio conditioning. Many people who avoid aerobics say they do so because the sessions have become too "dancey" and they think they can't keep up. There's nothing more embarrassing: everybody else is moving together in synchrony . . . and then there's you. You grapevine left while the rest of the class grapevines right. You power-jack up while the class power-jacks down. It's enough to push you back to that boring stationary bike, where fancy footwork is not requisite. If you were to give aerobics a fair chance, though, you would get better—I promise. I know; I was there.

> Measure your progress in inches, not just pounds. I had a brief moment of despair when I had my annual physical this year and I had gained three pounds. My clothes fit fine and I can even tell I've lost a little in my legs, which means my thighs now cover only *one* zip code. My doctor assured me that because I work out every day, I was losing fat and building muscle—which weighs more than fat.

You know something? It wasn't as bad as I thought. Nobody cared whether I knew the steps or that I was completely out of breath after the first three minutes of a sixty-minute workout. I realized that all of them had been panting in the back row once, too. And with every session I dared to attend, the class became easier. Eventually even I knew most of the steps and I was freed up to enjoy the music, which distracted me from the hard work I was doing.

If you fear the aerobics room more than your next root canal, here are things you can do to get past the dread. (This applies to kick-boxing, Tai Bo, and spinning, too.)

> "There is no failure except in no longer trying."
> —Elbert Hubbard

• *Forget about image.* Nobody else in the class really cares if you get out of step unless you keep crashing into them. If you can, avoid classes held between the peak hours of five and seven P.M. Try to attend those with fewer students so there's plenty of room for faux pas.

• *Expect to be clumsy at first.* Would you be disappointed if you didn't dance *en pointe* after one ballet class? Even advanced aerobicizers misstep when they attend a class given by someone other than their usual instructor.

• *Don't be shy about nabbing a spot up front near the instructor.* You can see his or her movements better. Plus you won't be watching a class full of people you think are more graceful than you are.

Did You Know?

Yankee Stadium was built in the 1920s. Fifty years later, when it was renovated, its seating capacity was reduced by 9,000 seats because the average American's bottom had increased four inches in width.

THE LUCKY THIRTEEN: TIPS FOR STICKING WITH IT

1. Identify potential reasons why you would skip exercise.
2. Find a role model.
3. Use a portable tape player if you work out alone.
4. Set your exercise clothes by the exit door at your house to prompt yourself to go to the gym at lunchtime.
5. Make appointments to exercise with friends.

6. Try a variety of programs to avoid boredom. Cross-training is the name of the game.
7. Don't push yourself too hard.
8. Set up a reward system for yourself.
9. Keep a log of the times you've exercised.
10. Seek out information on health and fitness.
11. Use affirmations—they make it easier to establish new habits.
12. If you miss a day, forgive yourself and get back to your routine as soon as possible. Beating yourself up accomplishes nothing.
13. Begin to see and talk about yourself as someone who is pursuing health. Even though extra weight takes a while to come off, you're working on it. Give yourself credit!

Did You Know?

If you walk forty-five minutes a day five days a week, you are half as likely to be sick with colds or the flu as those who are not exercising.

Recommended Reading

Two of my favorite books regarding exercise, health, and fitness are *Make the Connection* by Bob Green and Oprah Winfrey (Hyperion, 1996) and *Regaining the Power of Youth at Any Age* by Kenneth H. Cooper, M.D. (Nelson, 1998).

About Appearance

Appearances are deceiving. Appearances are in the eye of the beholder. We've all known attractive women who look in the mirror and see something different from what we do; that something may be a horror-movie monster, her mother on her worst day, or a "videotape" left over from childhood. Whatever they're seeing and why, they don't see what we do: attractive people. Not super-models, mind you—just ordinary, attractive human beings. We're probably all guilty of this misperception at certain times.

We need to practice changing our attitude toward our physical appearance.

FEELING GOOD ABOUT YOUR BODY

- Each time you look in a mirror, notice something attractive about your appearance. Be patient with yourself—this could take a while.
- Force yourself to turn away from the mirror if you spend all of your time criticizing your appearance.
- Forget comparing yourself to other women. You are you, not anyone else.
- Refrain from criticizing or even commenting on another woman's appearance.
- Remember that "comfortable and classic" is easier to fit into than "fashionable and trendy."
- Watch how the media portray women's bodies and their appearances. Avoid media that make you feel bad about the way you look.
- Learn to value and focus on things other than your appearance.
- Make a list of your ten best physical characteristics. Post it somewhere you'll see it often.

LOOK AND FEEL BETTER:
TWENTY-TWO WAYS TO PERK UP YOUR APPEARANCE

1. Give yourself a facial once a week. Your skin will be healthier and begin to glow.

2. Get a new haircut.

3. Smile at yourself in the mirror. Smiling is good for us, and it uses a lot fewer muscles than frowning does.

4. Get your nails done, even if it's not a special occasion. Or offer to trade manicures with a friend.

5. Expand your wardrobe by trading with a friend. Go through each other's closets. You probably both have things you seldom wear.

6. Paint your toenails.

7. Ask a younger friend or a professional cosmetologist to give you some tips on makeup.

8. Schedule a regular time, at least once a week, to spend an hour pampering yourself. The relaxation alone will perk up your appearance.

9. Get moving! Take a brisk walk the first chance you get. Your cheeks will be rosier.

10. If you're feeling ugly, make silly faces at yourself in the mirror until you laugh out loud. It's good to stretch your face muscles.

11. Take a nap—even if it's a short one—in the middle of the day. You'll feel and look better.

12. Brush your hair a hundred times.

13. Invest in a lighted makeup mirror.

14. Find a perfume you like and wear it.

15. Sliced cucumbers are great eye refreshers. Lie back with a slice on each eyelid for a few minutes.

16. Pull yourself up to your full height. Don't hunch or slouch. You'll feel better and look better, too.

17. Wear colors you feel good in. Your confidence will show.

18. Allow yourself the time and expense to get a massage or use the sauna and/or hot tub at a gym.

19. Get unwanted body hair waxed.

> "Why not be oneself? That is the whole secret of a successful appearance. If one is a greyhound, why try to look like a Pekinese?"
> —Dame Edith Sitwell

20. Indulge in fragrant body lotions, soaps, and bath powder. When you smell beautiful, you feel more beautiful.

21. If you wear glasses, look into investing in a more up-to-date or flattering pair, even if your prescription hasn't changed. (Since women who wear glasses usually wear them every day, if you apply the cost-per-wear wardrobe rule, they're not that expensive.)

22. Splurge on a session or two with a personal trainer. She can help you set fitness goals and tone up those trouble spots. Many Ys offer free personal training sessions for members.

Finding Your Style

- Shop around in stores you like and find a personal shopper or salesclerk you sense is honest and pleasant to be around. Stick with her. Or go shopping with a friend whose style you like and judgment you trust.
- Peruse mail-order catalogs and find ones that fit your taste.
- Discover the brands that fit you well—in size and taste.
- When you shop, wear panty hose and your usual amount of makeup, and fix your hair as usual. If you're shopping for a nice dress, take a pair of heels with you. If you're looking for summer vacation clothes, take sandals.
- Make sure the clothes you buy are returnable. When you get home, see how they look and feel in the comfort of your own bedroom in front of your own mirror. What else do they go with in your closet?

The Bottom Line

- Every day do at least one thing to become your physical best in terms of food, exercise, and appearance. And don't let these items fall to the bottom of your to-do list. To be our physical best is a lifelong, daily process. It takes trial and error, failure and forgiveness, and strong desire. Do one thing to take care of your physical self, then another. Soon you'll find it's growing on you—in a good way!

- Your physical best means *your* physical best—not Jane Fonda's, your next-door neighbor's, or that of a woman half your age. Accept who you are.

- Give up dieting for an eat-smart lifestyle. Know your body and what it needs.

- Look in your daily routine for hidden opportunities to exercise.

- Give yourself permission to try new things, and vary your exercise routine. Cross-training is the name of the game.

- Practice looking your best. Know what you look and feel good in—in terms of clothes and makeup.

- See yourself as a work in progress.

SEVEN

A Smarter, Sharper You

"You must learn day by day, year by year, to broaden your
horizon."
                                                —Ethel Barrymore

Life is one big, long learning curve. None of us ever gets it all
down. And wouldn't life be boring if there were nothing
new to learn? We owe it to our children and ourselves to
stay on top of things. If we stop growing today, we stop teaching
tomorrow. Learning should be a daily practice, and it's not confined to universities or books. By always asking "How can I improve?" a family manager is not just enhancing her own life, she's
passing on an invaluable attitude to her children.

From experience, I know it's all too easy to put our brains on the
shelf. We're so busy making sure the kids pass math that our own
mental growth gets pushed to the end of the to-do list. If we're not
careful, our husbands and social circle will grow without us.

There is something deeply satisfying about learning new things,
whether it's finding out that the ruby-throated hummingbird you
and your two-year-old watch out your kitchen window moves at
two hundred wing beats per second, mastering some basic French
so you can communicate with your new-to-America neighbor, or
programming your VCR (which for me ranks right up there with
molecular biology).

Years ago when my kids were young I read a quote by E. Stanley Jones that left me shaking in my boots: "You don't grow old. You get old by not growing." At that point in my life I realized that I could

> "One can remain alive . . . if one is unafraid of change, insatiable in intellectual curiosity, interested in big things and happy in small ways." —Edith Wharton

recite many of Bert and Ernie's lines, and I'd memorized the names of all the characters in Mister Rogers's neighborhood, but I feared the shelf life of my brain might expire if I didn't make a conscious effort to pursue a higher level of learning. I set a goal and gave myself permission and time to learn new things on a daily basis. Today I feel more confident about attempting new tasks, making decisions, and carrying on conversations with people whose intellects I admire. I am also more open to different ways of accomplishing everyday tasks and to new ideas. A commitment to lifelong learning causes you and me to get continually better as we get older.

The Secret of Growing Older and Better

Whether you're twenty-five or sixty-five, we all have two things in common: we will all be older next week than we are this week, and we will not be the same next week as we are this week.

Life does not stand still. We are constantly changing. In the past hour each of our bodies made a trillion trillion atoms. Our minds are constantly changing as well. The choices we make every hour of every day will make the difference as to whether we are older *and* better next week than we are this week. And not only next week, but next month and next year as well.

There's an art to growing intellectually while growing old. We won't automatically become interesting, vivacious senior citizens

> "The excitement of learning separates youth from old age. As long as you're learning, you're not old."
> —Rosalyn S. Yalow

the day our first social security check arrives. A lifetime commitment to making our days count, rather than merely counting our days, starts now—wherever we are. How we spend our time in our twenties, thirties, forties, and fifties will determine what we'll be like in our sixties, seventies, eighties, and nineties. Sometimes it's hard to remember this when you have a baby pulling at your pants leg, a grade schooler participating in every activity available, a teenager fighting peer pressure, a husband in midlife crisis, and a boss who expects you to say "How high?" when he says "Jump." I have to keep reminding myself that I have immeasurably more to offer to those who need me when I take time to develop myself.

Seven Smart Reasons for Becoming a Lifelong Learner

1. Learning leads to learning, and you'll discover interests you never knew you had.
2. You'll feel a sense of accomplishment and a commensurate increase in self-esteem that will help carry you through the hard times.
3. You'll have something to think about when you're stuck in traffic.
4. You'll have more data in your personal hard drive, a.k.a. your brain, to draw from when you need to solve a problem.
5. You'll be better, more interesting company for yourself.
6. You'll seldom be bored because you can find things to learn wherever you are.
7. You'll model the value of learning for your children, and they get all these benefits as well.

A Minute Found Can Be a New Thing Learned

When I made a resolution to be an interesting person to myself, to Bill, and to others, Ms. Mediocrity immediately reared her ugly head: "I don't have a big block of time to take a class or read extensively or take an apprenticeship." Over time I realized that I was fooling myself with that objection. I knew that I could find time for the truly important things; it just depended on how high a priority I gave them. I decided to pay attention and seize the day, though in my case it was often seize the minutes. I began grabbing moments that otherwise would have been wasted and set up some new routines that have served me well. As it turns out, I also learned that little chunks of time are just as valuable as big blocks.

Now I always carry something to read with me on appointments. I clip magazine articles and save newsletters in a plastic portfolio in the car so I'll have them when I'm stalled in traffic or waiting for baseball practice to end. (Do you know that the average person spends twenty-seven hours a year sitting at traffic lights?) I work crossword puzzles on airplanes. I listen to books on tape while I drive from errand to errand.

When I started to improve my mind and expand my horizons, I began to collect odd bits of information. I made a list of topics that interested me and began collecting articles, statistics, and quotes on these subjects. Little did I know that this information would be part of my books someday. (How do you think I knew the average amount of time people spend sitting at stoplights?)

Sometimes we think that what we learn is more important than the fact that

> "I expect I shall be a student to the end of my days."
> —Anton Chekhov

we're learning. For example, we decide that learning computer programming is better than learning about early childhood development. And if we must learn about early childhood development, we feel we should learn it in a university setting rather than in the labs we have right at home.

Top Ten Logjams to Learning

1. *Procrastinating.* Putting learning off until a less busy day in the future is in reality a decision to neglect it altogether. You know life will never be less busy—you'll just have different duties. Start today.

2. *Not following through.* This is a cousin to procrastination, another situation in which good intentions are worth nothing until you act on them.

3. *Not being prepared.* You may need to do a little homework, paperwork, or plotting to make learning a priority. If you want to finish that nursing degree, for example, you'll have to find out how many of your college credits from fifteen years ago will transfer to the college you now live near. If you want to take advantage of opportunities to read, you'll have to locate some good reading material and make sure it's handy when you have time for it.

4. *Knowing it all already.* It's easy to assume that since we function fairly well in our daily lives, we know as much as we need to. But no one knows what challenges will arise tomorrow that will call for new knowledge or the ability to assimilate new information. We do ourselves a favor by deciding that there's always more to know.

5. *Having unrealistic expectations.* When we assume we can pick up a new skill immediately, absorb as much information at a time as our brainy best friend, or master a new concept in weeks, we set ourselves up for failure. As in all other areas, we need to allow ourselves some slack at the same time we give

ourselves the gift of learning. Each of us processes information in her own way—and that's okay.

6. *Quitting too soon.* Becoming discouraged is a constant threat. See 5.

7. *Not learning from our mistakes.* Our failures, large or small, are some of our best teachers. We need to take advantage of the education our mistakes offer us.

8. *Playing it too safe.* Staying within our well-known circles out of fear limits not only our knowledge but our personalities. What is predictable is often—you guessed it!—boring. No one wants to be dull! (What have you always wanted to learn more about? Step out and do it!) If everybody had always done only what they already knew how to do, we might still be living in caves and cooking over open fires.

9. *Assuming our energy would be better spent elsewhere.* Besides limiting us to spending our energy on things we "should" be doing (and presumably already know how to do), this approach means a life of all work and no play. It makes Jane a very dull girl.

10. *Allowing unsupportive people to discourage you.* Perhaps your family or social group underestimates the value of learning new things or acquiring knowledge. Maybe they dishearten you in such pursuits. If this is the case, you need to remember that learning is a personal choice. Why do *you* think it is important? Sometimes you have to be your own advocate.

LEARNING BEGINS WITH QUESTIONS

Ask yourself the following questions:

- What is the best book I've ever read? Why?
- What are five topics I've always wanted to know more about?

> "Education is a private matter between the person and the world of knowledge and experience." —Lillian Smith

- What are five things I'd like to learn to do?
- What things do I enjoy and do well?
- Are there areas or skills I would like to enhance or improve?

Asking ourselves questions points us in the direction we might want to go. Get yourself a small notebook for your learning journey. When you come across a topic or a bit of information that piques your interest, jot down a question to yourself. Keep a running list of books that sound interesting, even if you think it will be a while before you get to them.

Start where you are. Are there other books by the same author or on the same topic you might read? Check them out of the library or buy them, and then set aside fifteen or twenty minutes a day to read them.

"Book learning," if that's what you call new information, doesn't always have to come from books. I carry a notebook with me almost everywhere I go. When I meet someone new—on an airplane, standing in a long line, or at a dinner—I try to learn about his/her interests and areas of expertise. Since most people like to share what they know, I've learned a lot. Like the best mountains to climb in Colorado. What big companies like to see on a college grad's résumé. Good Chardonnays. Where to eat in New York City, Los Angeles, and Minneapolis. Savvy travel tips. What's new in software. Ideas for funding a business.

Learning something new can directly affect our lives and work as family managers. For example, I've known women to whom organization didn't come naturally. For them, a workshop with an expert on organization might be a learning experience that has a beneficial effect on their and their families' lives. We can always learn more, even when we're good at some-

> "Learn from everyone."
> —Ben Franklin

thing and interested in it. I've heard more than one family manager who likes to cook tell me she's been energized and learned new things by taking a cooking class. It's obvious how a low-fat gourmet cooking class might positively affect a family's life.

Caution: As our knowledge grows, so does our appetite for learning. Soon you may have to get a bigger notebook!

Give Yourself Credit

When you think about taking on a learning project, do you have trouble coming up with things you'd like to learn to do? Or do you run into a brick wall of no time and too many commitments? If so, it might be time to take stock.

What have you learned in the past six months? It might have been how to use a new software program at work or how to potty-train your toddler. What did you feel like when you knew the task or the deadline was looming? What steps did you take to find out the information you needed to know? What did you discover that you didn't expect to discover?

You are a learner even if you don't think of yourself that way. Asking ourselves questions like these can remind us what pleasure we got from learning new things, what obstacles we encountered, and how we dealt with those obstacles. The answers to those questions can lead us down new learning paths. If you were frustrated by the software program, perhaps you know you *don't* want to take a computer programming class at your community college. Maybe you also know that you don't want to stay in a job that requires you to be at the computer several hours a day. So what you know is that you can (because you did) learn one new skill. What are others you might want to learn?

But maybe you got your information about different potty-training techniques off the Internet. If that was the first time you have used that huge resource, give yourself credit, and not just for getting good information. Then ask yourself what else you could use your new research skills for.

List five or ten new things you've learned in the last month.

1. _____

2. _____

3. _____

4. _____

5. _____

6. _____

7. _____

8. _____

9. _____

10. _____

Smart Is as Smart Does

I used to feel stupid when people told me things—new information, names, how to do something—and I'd promptly forget them. Bill and I had plenty of tense marital moments when he would tell me five times how to save files in my computer and I wouldn't retain the information. Finally I realized I had to *do* it to learn it.

When I read about learning styles, I realized I am a visual and kinesthetic learner. I need to see and do. I used to think only old people had to write things down in order to remember them. Not so!

Now that I know this about myself, I can compensate. I write down new people's names as soon as I can. When someone gives me instructions verbally, I either take notes as I'm hearing them or envision myself following the instructions: press this button, then that one.

Seven Kinds of Smart

You're at least one of these—more likely a combination of several. Identify the kinds of learning that are most effective for you. Then use them as guides to choosing your methods for lifelong learning.

1. *Word smart:* Learns by listening, reading, writing, and speaking
2. *Logic smart:* Learns by using numbers, facts, and scientific principles, and by observing and experimenting
3. *Picture smart:* Sees what casual observers miss, can visualize and can use these powers to create images and concrete structures
4. *Music smart:* Grasps information that's presented melodically; understanding is enhanced when materials are presented in song
5. *Body smart:* Learns through senses and movement
6. *People smart:* Learns through social process, by talking with others, picking up on verbal and nonverbal clues and relationships
7. *Self smart:* Learns through introspection, by sitting and thinking about things

> "Everything is data. But data isn't everything."
> —Pauline Bart

Practices to Get You in Practice

- Keep a list of things you want to learn about.
- Keep an ongoing list of books you want to read.
- Read with a highlighter pen to mark thoughts you want to remember and ideas that pique your interest.
- When you encounter something you don't know, jot it down in your notebook so you remember to look it up later.
- Invest in some reference books for your home library.
- Listen to books on tape.
- If you have a CD-ROM on your computer, buy some reference materials. It's easy to find what you're looking for. Plus, researching one thing often leads to learning about/researching another.
- Learn how to change a flat tire.
- Call your local community college or university and ask them to send you a catalog for evening extension classes.
- Watch the newspaper for events or lectures you might be interested in. Put them on your schedule.
- Tell your friends when you want to learn something about a specific topic or topics. They can be great research assistants, leading you to books, classes, and other information.
- Search the Internet for subjects you want to learn about. You have a universe of information right at your fingertips.
- Protect your learning time. Get in the habit of setting aside a few minutes every day to learn something. Read the newspaper or a book, or just think. Don't be surprised if that few minutes grows to every spare minute.

Fun Learning Stuff

- Work crossword puzzles.
- Play Trivial Pursuit or other games that introduce you to new facts.

- Play chess or other strategy games.
- Play word games. Scrabble, Boggle, and 25 Words or Less are all good commercial games. You can play the Dictionary Game with just a dictionary, some notepads and pencils, and three cohorts. One person looks up a word in the dictionary and announces it. (If anyone knows the real definition, choose another word.) Each person makes up a definition for the word and writes it down. The person holding the dictionary writes the correct definition. He or she reads them all aloud, and the players guess which one is correct. You earn points if someone picks your fictional definition or if you guess the right one.
- Listen to classical music. Read the liner notes on the CD. Begin at the beginning and work your way through to the twentieth century.
- Make up stories with your kids that use new words or facts you read in the morning paper. (You can do this even with small children.) Use the add-on method. One person starts, leaving the story hanging in midsentence, and the next person adds to it.
- Play memory games with your kids in the car. The classic one is an alphabet game. It starts, "I went to Grandma's house [or wherever you want] and took [something that starts with an A]." The next person repeats the A word, and adds a B word, and so on through the alphabet, always repeating what came before. Or memorize state capitals or the presidents in order.
- Rent how-to videos and together learn a new skill or about a different country or culture.
- If you and/or your spouse like to read aloud and/or be read to, set aside a half an hour or an hour a week when the kids are in bed. Turn the phone off. Read each other favorite poems. Read Shakespeare or anything that pleases both of you and that you might not otherwise read.

The breakfast table is the perfect environment for everyone in your family to grow in mind, body, and spirit. Don't get me wrong. We're not the Cleavers. We're a typical busy family. But mornings have always struck me as a potentially rich time for personal development—both for myself and for my family—in five to six minutes over cold cereal, a bagel, fruit juice, and multivitamins. We learn a fact a day from a book such as *The Dictionary of Cultural Literacy*, which is currently sitting on our table, a word-a-day calendar, or the morning newspaper. We're eating, which is of course creating physical energy to face the day. We say a prayer for our day, establishing a spiritual perspective. We ask about each other's agenda for the day, and we encourage each other to do our best—adding to family closeness and individual success.

Word Up

When I was a child, I watched for the mail carrier to deliver my mom's *Reader's Digest* every month. I immediately turned to "It Pays to Increase Your Word Power," a little feature that had (and still has) several words with multiple-choice answers. It was like taking a test without the pressure to perform. And I learned new words. Here are some other ideas:

> "Knowledge is essential to conquest: only according to our ignorance are we helpless. Thought creates character. Character dominates conditions."   —Annie Besant

- Learn more about the English language by learning a Latin-based language such as Spanish, French, or Italian.
- When you read or hear a word you don't under-

stand, look it up. Try to use it in conversation so you commit it to memory.

> "Study as if you were going to live forever. Live as if you were going to die tomorrow."
> —Maria Mitchell

- Keep a list of new words you learn.
- When you look up a word in the dictionary, take a few extra minutes to browse. Look up related words, or just read a few entries that catch your eye.
- Invest in a good thesaurus.

Creating a Learning Atmosphere

- Designate a favorite armchair or spot in your home for reading. You'll enjoy going there and will be more likely to keep reading if it's a pleasant experience.
- Set up a writing corner. Keep your journal there.
- Keep several pens, notebooks, drawing paper, and art supplies handy. If you feel moved to stretch your creative powers by writing, drawing, or painting, it helps to have supplies on hand.
- Ask for books on topics you're interested in for holiday or birthday presents.
- Create a learning idea file. Clip interesting articles, stories, and facts and figures and put them all in one place. Periodically review it.
- Subscribe to at least one weekly newsmagazine and one general-interest monthly so you'll keep up with current events, ideas, books, and movies.

Be a Student of People

It's been said of Will Rogers that he never met a stranger. Well, the same is true of my father. He taught me that when we approach people with an open mind, we learn things from them. We can be a student of anyone—our husband, son, or daughter; an aunt; a friend. All we need to do is ask them questions about their day: what they learned, what they liked, what they hated.

Five Tips for Being a Good Listener

1. Ask the question and then let the person speak. Don't interrupt.
2. Respond by summarizing what you heard.
3. If you don't understand something or want him or her to tell you more, ask.
4. Don't offer advice or solutions that people don't ask for.
5. Ask open-ended questions such as "What do you do in an average day?" You learn more than you would from those that can be answered simply, such as "Did you have a good day?"

When we take the attitude that we can learn from everyone we meet, we will.

Stretch Yourself

Ask what-if questions of yourself and others. What if you could meet anyone from history? Which three people would you choose to dine with? What if you had enough money to quit working? What if you could fly? What-ifs stretch the imagination and sometimes lead to whole new paths in life.

You Can Because You Must

I don't know about you, but my crystal ball is not in good working order. I have a friend whose second grader came home one day and proudly announced she'd written her first computer program. "How old were you when you wrote your first computer program?" she asked her mother. My friend explained that the first computer she ever saw in her life was on a high school science field trip. It filled an entire room and was run by men in white jackets. Nobody had even dreamed of personal computers then.

Today my friend, like many of her peers, doesn't write computer programs. But she uses them every day in her work. "Who would've thought this fifteen or even ten years ago?" she asked me.

That got me thinking about how we take things we do know for granted. I also use a computer just about every day. I use the Internet just about every day. I also use a fax machine, voice mail, and a cellular phone. I know how to use these things. I take them for granted.

Make a list of the things you use with skill and ease every day—or at least frequently—that you'd never heard of when you were young. You learned all of that. What can you learn next?

Let me tell you, I think anyone who can learn to operate a microwave oven, a food processor, or a space-age vacuum cleaner can learn to navigate the Internet. Recently I went to the library to look for books on business management. I hadn't done a research project like this for a long time. I was amazed. What used to take a half an hour of moving from card-catalog drawer to card-catalog drawer took about two minutes to find through the online catalog. I had my books and was on my way in no time.

The thing is, though we often learn things only when we have to, we need to realize we *always* have to. For our own sakes as well as our families'.

Stretch Yourself

Buy a do-it-yourself manual on something, anything that you don't already know how to do. Read it. Decide if you want to do it. Do it.

Double Your Learning Pleasure

There's a lot of talk about "multitasking" these days. I don't know who invented that concept, but I wouldn't be surprised if a busy family manager did. It's a matter of survival. The following ideas are means to grow in at least two of the following ways—mind, body, spirit—at the same time.

- Take a class on low-fat desserts.
- Buy your favorite books on tape and listen to them when you are walking. If you've ever had the experience of not being able to put a book down, the benefits of this are clear. An extra twenty minutes of walking will seem like nothing.
- When you are dealing with PMS, pregnancy, menopause, or a chronic illness, it helps to know more. Read a book. Go to a one-day workshop—these are often sponsored by HMOs or hospitals. For a nominal fee some major medical centers will allow you to order journal articles on specific topics. Or ask your physician to recommend books. Learning all you can about your condition will help you know how to care for your body in wise ways.
- If you're thinking of starting a new exercise program, do a little research. What should you do if you want to build muscle mass? Increase your endurance? Finding out will build your

intellectual strength as well as enable you to build yourself up physically.

> "Wear the old coat and buy the new book."   —Austin Phelps

- Be a tourist in your own town. Take a walking tour of your city or one near you.
- Learn a new sport, such as golf. You'll find out how to relax, concentrate, and improve hand-eye coordination, and have a new subject to talk to the folks in the office about. Other ideas: swimming, kick-boxing, dancing.
- Take a guided nature hike.
- Look into classes or book groups at a church, synagogue, or community center.

The Bottom Line

- Learning is a lifelong activity that directly affects our roles as family managers and our attitude about our whole life.
- Learning new things increases our skills and confidence and leads to more learning.
- Practice learning wherever you are, whenever you can—in small chunks of time while you wait, on airplanes, in everyday situations.
- Give yourself credit for what you're learning.
- Periodically assess your interests and what you think you would like to learn more about. Then go for it! Read books on the subject or enroll in a class.

EIGHT

Less Stress for You

"A sad soul can kill you far quicker than a germ."
—John Steinbeck

You leave your office at five-thirty, hop into your late-model sports car, and ease onto the freeway, where there are few vehicles but yours. When you arrive home, your husband greets you at the door with a refreshing drink and tells you he took off from work early and let the sitter go home. He reports that he picked up around the house, fed and bathed the kids, and put a beef tenderloin in the oven. You walk into your children's rooms, where they are quietly playing with toys. They give you a warm hug, tell you they love you, and nicely ask you to read them a short book. After spending this quality time with them, you soak in a fragrant bubble bath for twenty minutes, slip into something sexy, then enjoy a quiet candlelit dinner with your husband.

"I hate it when my food touches! My applesauce is touching my chicken." Jolted back to reality, you begin to scrape the applesauce off of the chicken. Thoughts of beef tenderloin and candlelight fade away. After dinner you clear a path through the family room, throw in a load of laundry, separate two squabbling kids, and run their bathwater. You ask your husband if he thinks your car will make it past 120,000 miles—it stalled again today in rush-hour

traffic. Your head is pound-
ing. You feel stressed and
you wonder how much more
you can take.

Sound familiar? Our sto-
ries may vary a bit, but we

> "There are two ways of meeting
> difficulties: You alter the
> difficulties, or you alter yourself
> to meet them."
> —Phyllis Bottome

probably all have at least one thing in common: we'd like less
stress in our lives.

Many of us have made the reduction of stress our Holy Grail.
We act on it constantly. We change jobs, spouses, and neighbor-
hoods. We pay therapists and sip herbal teas. We get massages. We
practice aromatherapy, take pills, and read books. We meditate.
We go on retreats where our inner child can indulge in all the temper tantrums she wants. We follow gurus, and we look for be-all
and end-all solutions to eliminate stress from our lives—once and
for all.

The trouble is, avoiding stress isn't really possible. It's part of
being human. The word *stress* itself describes an entirely normal psychophysiological process—our body and emotions working
together—without which we would die. Dr. Hans Selye, who is
known as the father of stress research, defines stress as "the non-
specific response of the body to any demand made upon it."

Now wait a minute, I said to myself when I read Dr. Selye's definition. I thought stress was getting stuck in bumper-to-bumper
traffic on the way to the airport or a baby vomiting on my new
white silk blouse or a clerk telling me—and the six people waiting
in line behind me—that my credit card has been rejected or the
highway department calling to tell me my son has been in an acci-
dent and has been taken to the hospital.

Contrary to popular belief, stress is not the situation; it is our
response to the situation. Stress is the reaction we have when
small irritations or big catastrophes enter our lives. Stress is also

> "No one can live without experiencing some degree of stress. You may think that only serious disease or intensive physical or mental injury can cause stress. This is false. . . . Stress is also the spice of life, for any emotion, any activity, causes stress."   —Hans Selye

the reaction we have when something really wonderful happens in our lives. It doesn't make much difference if the situation we react to is a positive one, such as buying a new house, or a negative one, such as going through a divorce. Although the end result of negative stress can be very different from that of rewarding stress—high blood pressure, a weakened immune system, heart disease, arthritis, to name a few—our initial bodily response is similar in both cases.

Our bodies are constantly in change mode, adapting to what's going on around us. This is an incredibly sophisticated process, more intricate than we imagine. My best friend, Dr. Kathryn Waldrep, tells me that stress involves our brain and nervous system, the heart and circulatory system, the liver and spleen, and the adrenal glands and immune system, and that it should not be taken lightly. When we have too much stress for too long, damage can result.

So what does this mean to you and me, overly busy women juggling numerous jobs and responsibilities while at the same time trying to enjoy some modicum of peace and fulfillment as human beings? In my mind it means living smart. It means that we have an accurate view of reality and—no matter how much we try to deny what's going on in the world or practice positive thinking—understand that we live in a stressful world to begin with. Dr. Richard Swenson puts it like this: "No one in the history of humankind has ever had to live with the stressors we have acting upon us today. They are unprecedented. . . . Exponential change is one stressor we dare not underestimate. Universal indebtedness, hurry, noise, complexity, and schedule overload are crushing stressors. Both parents working stresses the parents, the family unit, and the children. . . . Stress disorders are experienced in nearly every household."

In addition to the state of our culture, we all have hidden stressors in our lives. The body adjusts to operating at an increased level of stress in response to stress-producing factors we don't even know exist—or at least we don't recognize them as being stress-producing. Our bodies have the remarkable ability to adjust to a wide variety of conditions. For example, if you walk out of the bright sunlight into a dark room, at first you can discern nothing. But then your eyes get used to the darkness, and very soon you can see clearly. But there's a negative side to our bodies' ability to adapt. Our bodies will adapt to situations that in the long run are harmful to us. Although you may not realize it, any of the following could be causing you stress right now without your knowing it.

- cartoons blaring from the family TV
- your teenager's stereo system
- living near a noisy freeway, train line, or airport
- bad lighting
- an uncomfortable desk chair
- dogs barking
- violence on the evening news
- a drawer that comes off the track every time you open it
- clutter
- a never-diminishing pile of laundry to be ironed
- the mail
- tight-fitting clothes
- a spouse who won't talk
- remodeling or construction
- dirty house
- change in pay or hours
- problems with your car
- difficulty sleeping
- illness in family
- houseguests
- indebtedness
- sexual difficulty
- anger toward your spouse
- anger toward your children
- trouble with in-laws
- weather conditions

Any or all of these (and you no doubt can add many to the list) can be the source of subtle, continuous, and potentially harmful stress, without our even being aware that they are causing us discomfort. Our bodies adapt to the stress by producing more adrenaline, which blots out the discomfort and gives us a false sense of well-being. When this happens, we realize that little things that once didn't faze us now set us off. We may have trouble relaxing or feel like a human pressure cooker—always ready to blow our top. There may also be physical signs that we're experiencing too much stress—an ulcer, headaches, or high blood pressure. Now is a good time to stop and ask yourself these questions:

1. Is my body trying to tell me something right now?
2. Am I avoiding being honest about something in my life?
3. Are there things I can do right now that will make a positive difference?

What Pulls Your Trigger?

We all have different triggers that set us off. What may stress me to the max may not bother you at all. What deeply upsets you may be the least of my worries. We're all unique in terms of what stressors lead to knots in our stomach or black moods, but we all have them. In my case, I can usually write books and magazine articles on deadline without breaking a sweat. I can give a speech to a thousand women and not blink an eye. I can present large-scale proposals to high-powered executives and remain cool, calm, and collected. But tell

> "Researchers strongly agree on two basic principles: first, that man has limited capacity; and second, that overloading the system leads to serious breakdown of performance."
> —Alvin Toffler

me to bake a cake from
scratch for the bake sale at
school, and I'm likely to break
out in hives, ingest large doses
of antacid, and/or come down
with a stress-induced headache.

> "Great events make me quiet
> and calm; it is only trifles that
> irritate my nerves."
> —Queen Victoria

You know what pulls your chain.

SIGNS THAT YOU ARE STRESSED

These are symptoms of serious stress. If you have more than two,
it's time to make some changes.

- frequent anger or irritation over little things
- withdrawal from friends and family
- difficulty getting along with others
- frequent colds and more health problems than usual
- continual worry and fatigue
- loss of interest in normal activities
- overwork
- trouble sleeping
- blaming others
- difficulty concentrating
- hearing but not listening
- fear of making decisions
- general lack of enjoyment and satisfaction in life
- reckless behavior, such as driving too fast, eating too much
  or too fast, or drinking too much
- feeling trapped without choices

We all feel stressed from time to time, but sometimes life is
more than we can handle. If you feel like this, give yourself permission to seek help. See your regular physician or call your pastor or rabbi for recommendations of a counselor or mental health

professional. Remember, just as if you're hiring a plumber or a babysitter, you are hiring someone to help you.

Weathering Emotional Storms

Bill and I spent a week last summer with our three boys on Florida's Gulf Coast. One day we anchored a friend's boat near the beach of a lovely island. We walked the beach and picked up seashells until our swimsuit-clad bodies began turning an unhealthy shade of crimson. It was early afternoon and the sun was hot, so we jumped into the boat and headed back to the house where we were staying.

As we steered the boat away from the island and headed east, we noticed that we could not even see one of the bridges we would pass on our way back. A sudden, unexpected storm had come up about a mile ahead of us, and we were headed right into it. Lightning danced across the sky and the waves grew bigger and bigger. Thankfully, there was a marina close by, and we pulled into its harbor to wait the storm out.

As I stood in a small shelter on the shore waiting for the sky to clear again, I thought about how, if you're not paying attention to the weather, you can get yourself into a life-and-death situation in a boat. As the lightning flashed around me, a lightbulb went on in my head: our emotional weather is a lot like the weather outside. It's predictable, to a certain extent. But even with satellites and computers, meteorologists admit they can't know for certain when the weather is going to change and what conditions will cause it to shift. Some days I wake up with a sunny sense of well-being. I sail through the day, no matter what it brings, with patience, tolerance, and good humor. Nothing throws me.

Other days are partly cloudy. Maybe it will rain or snow. Maybe it won't. I may even be caught in a sudden storm. On partly cloudy emotional days, I might wake up feeling fine. But then James forgets his lunch or science project, so I have to interrupt my schedule and deliver it to school. One of my editors calls and says she needs

"I have so much to do that I am going back to bed."
—Samoyard proverb

major revisions on a magazine article—yesterday. Then there are three more phone calls, each demanding a response within twenty-four hours. On days like these, the size of the disruption doesn't matter. It could be a broken fingernail or a stubbed toe. My stress level rises and I'm thrown off course. The day has changed from partly cloudy to completely cloudy, grumpy, and going all wrong.

Then there are the days when I wake up and my emotional weather is severe. Think hurricane. Think tornado. Think flash flood. I'd really like to get a cup of coffee and a good book, and crawl back in bed.

Pick-Me-Ups for Partly Cloudy Days

1. Wear a favorite outfit. Bright colors make you feel better. Make sure it's something you'll like seeing on yourself in the mirror.
2. Take time to let yourself feel what you're feeling. We don't always have to know why we're down, although sometimes it helps. Have a cup of tea. Take ten minutes to examine your emotional weather.
3. Exercise, even if it's only twenty minutes of brisk walking.
4. Cry if you need to. Tears can be very cleansing.
5. Call a good friend. Just telling someone we love how we feel can help.
6. Take a short nap.
7. Eat smart. You need enduring energy today. Sugar highs and alcohol lows are not helpful.
8. Write down ten things you are thankful for.
9. Take time out to read part of a book that lifts your spirits.

10. Buy a ticket to a special event.
11. Paint a picture—even if you can't paint.
12. Start writing that book.
13. Have breakfast in bed.
14. Take a bubble bath.
15. Plan a vacation.
16. Put on some favorite music.
17. Open your windows and let in as much light as possible. If you don't have a nice view, put a vase full of colorful flowers on your windowsill.
18. Take some time to spruce up your desk or work environment. I keep favorite pictures of family and friends on my desk. I also have colorful office supplies and my favorite books close at hand.
19. Rearrange some furniture.
20. Clear a cluttered area that's causing you visual stress. Purging even a small area of papers or unwanted items can be refreshing.

Our emotional moods are affected by a lot of different factors, from what we eat to what hormones are raging to how much sleep we get. How we're getting along with our families—teething babies, petulant teenagers, spouses we don't get to spend enough quality time with—also affects our emotions. Unemployment, serious illness, and financial crises make their mark as well. In fact, myriad factors go into creating our emotional weather. And they're often interrelated. We need to pay attention to all the factors affecting our emotional weather. How we're eating, how much we're sleeping and exercising, what kinds of work we're doing, and what demands outside of work we're taking on all matter immensely. We need to identify the ones we can control and learn how to guide our own ship wherever possible.

> "Music hath charms to soothe the savage breast."
> —William Congreve

Refitting Our Reactions

Part of becoming personally successful, no matter what our dreams and goals, is learning to react to stress and deal with our emotions in healthy ways. The fact is, we can control the way stress affects our lives. While we can't always control what happens to us, we can choose how to react to it. Say the dreaded chicken pox visits your home. Three scratching children are whining in unison, but you have a choice: get mad or frustrated, which will increase your stress level (not to mention your kids'). Or lean into the challenge, accepting a temporary cutback in family (and/or work) routines, applying your energy to making the kids as comfortable as possible, and cutting yourself some slack in other areas.

The point is, we all have choices. Part of responding to stress is learning to see situations for what they are, not for what we imagine them to be. It's easy to blow things out of proportion, needlessly raising our stress level.

When the dog is vomiting on the new carpet, your ten-year-old has decided to cook dinner but needs help because she just dropped a jar of spaghetti sauce on the tile floor, your five- and seven-year-olds are starting World War III in the backyard, and your husband calls to say he's bringing his out-of-town colleague home for dinner, you could beat the dog, tell your daughter that only a stupid person would pick up a jar of sauce with wet hands, knock your boys' heads together to teach them that violence isn't a way to solve problems, and tell your husband that you're not running a restaurant and if you were, reservations would be required a week in advance. Then you could get in your car, drive to the airport, and fly to Paris.

Or you could call a time-out for everybody, including yourself, before dealing with the crises one at a time. During these few moments you could say a prayer for the ability to remain calm and not say anything you'll regret later.

Then you could tell your daughter you'll help her clean up the broken glass in a few minutes. Put the dog in the backyard with the boys, telling them to take care of her, thereby distracting their attention from the fight. Or if that doesn't work, send them off to their rooms for a quiet time. Get the dog's mess cleaned up before it starts to set. Ask your husband to stop for a bottle of wine, some French bread, and a chocolate cake on his way home. Tell him to take the long way, showing his work buddy the highlights of your town, buying yourself time to clean up the kitchen and pull something out of the freezer. (Not every family manager has a stocked freezer or pantry, ready for last-minute guests. But maybe you have the phone number of a ready-to-pop-in-the-oven gourmet grocery. If you're *really* lucky, there's one in your town that delivers.)

The point is, we do ourselves and our families a favor when we wisely and calmly meet the inevitable crises of life we face day in and day out.

Recently I had an opportunity to practice what I'm preaching. I invested in a new pair of summer sandals. (I use the word *invested* because the brands of shoes that fit my hard-to-fit feet don't fit our budget.) I wore them once and then, because I intended to take them with me to the alterations shop to wear when I was having a skirt hemmed, I put them in a bag on the floor of the bedroom, next to the wastepaper basket. Unfortunately, I didn't get the errand done before I had to leave town early the next morning.

That was a Friday—garbage collection day. So that morning, according to plan, Bill faithfully emptied the

> "You have to accept whatever comes, and the only important thing is that you meet it with courage and with the best that you have to give."
> —Eleanor Roosevelt

wastepaper basket in our bedroom and picked up the rumpled bag lying next to it, inserting it in the trash bag.

Good-bye, expensive new shoes! Hello, learning opportunity!

When something bad happens, we have three possible responses:

1. We can blame others. When I realized my shoes had gone to live at the city dump, my first response was to blame Bill. "The bag wasn't in the trash! You should have looked inside the bag first."

2. We can beat up on ourselves. I told myself if I hadn't been so busy I would have run the errand. Or if I had been more organized, I would have put the shoes away in the closet. After all, I'm the one who's always protesting about things strewn about the house, emphasizing that there is a place for everything and everything should be in its place. The conclusion I reached was that I was too stupid to follow my own routines.

3. Or we can make the best of the situation, seeing it for what it is without using our built-in situation-enlarger to blow it all out of proportion. After a few minutes of self-abuse, I came to. I realized nobody was dead or hurt. Nothing crucial to our lives was lost. I had made a mistake by leaving the shoes where they shouldn't have been. I did it because I was busy. But that didn't mean I was a bad person. Nor did it mean Bill was. And while I felt a pang at having lost the perfect summer shoes just at the beginning of the summer, I had other shoes and feet to wear them on. So what was the big deal? I could see the situation for what it

> "The art of being wise is the art of knowing what to overlook."
> —William James

was. Sometimes we have to go through the first two responses to get to the third.

Oddly enough, the shoe affair brought home a truth. Losing the
shoes gave me a chance to look at the difference between how I
see my life and myself and how I act on what I see. If the fact that
I made a mistake means to me that I'm incompetent, then I act on
that "reality." And I take my frustration out on those around me.
It's a lose-lose scenario. Instead, if after a mishap I focus on what's
really important and true—such as the truth that even the most organized people occasionally drop a stitch or two—then I can offer
myself some slack. In turn, I will extend that grace to those around
me. Again, my sense of well-being directly affects my family's.

For me, knowing that I can choose to have a healthy perspective
makes all the difference. I can turn lose/lose into win/win, depend-
ing on how I respond. Here are three strategies that can help.

1. Before you blame, count to ten. Recite the alphabet. Snap a
   rubber band on your wrist. Do whatever it takes to hold your
   tongue and keep reaction 1—blaming someone else—to
   yourself. (Note: This doesn't mean you can't or shouldn't
   lovingly and patiently confront people with how something
   they have done makes you feel.) Avoid sentences that start
   with *you*, as in "You always (or never) . . ." or "You should
   (or shouldn't) . . ."
2. Turn beating yourself up into a wallowing session. Go ahead.
   Blame yourself for whatever went wrong. Then blame yourself for the weather, the high price of coffee, the morning
   rush hour, the state of politics, and anything else you can
   think of—until you're laughing, or at least smiling. This exercise in exaggeration is aimed at making us see how we're
   not responsible for things we often take responsibility for.

And even if we *are* responsible for something like leaving the shoes in a bag near the trash, we've made a mistake, not caused a hurricane off the coast of Florida.

3. Jot down all the reasons you can think of why your mistake is not such a big deal. Keep the list where you can find it for future reference.

Strategies for Relieving Stress

I was personally inspired by the movie *Dances with Wolves.* The main character, John Dunbar, arrives at his frontier post in the middle of nowhere only to find it in total disarray. Instead of letting the circumstances dictate his disposition, he focuses on what he has and what he can do. He sees himself as responsible and capable. He disciplines himself to make the most of the situation and refuses to see himself as a victim, even though he is faced with insurmountable odds.

Whatever the insurmountable odds in our lives, there are always changes we can make and actions we can take that will help us better deal with stress and control our emotions. Here are some ideas to get you started.

- *Create buffer zones in your schedule.* When one is flying from Nashville to Los Angeles, the airlines allow only three minutes to change planes in Dallas. A much greater margin of error is needed. We would do well to do this in our life. If you have a busy schedule with nonstop appointments, create small buffer zones between them. Even ten minutes extra can defuse your tension.
- *Correct recurring frustrations when possible.* Six o'clock is the witching hour in many homes. Avoid the what's-for-dinner dilemma by getting the family involved on Sunday

night writing a menu for the coming week. Post it on the refrigerator so the first parent or older child who comes home
in the afternoon knows what to start for dinner. Also, keep
your pantry stocked with items you can prepare in a jiffy.
Write down nine or ten simple, favorite recipes and always
keep the ingredients on your master shopping list.

- *Avoid negative people.* Take a long walk at lunchtime instead
  of hanging out in the employee lunchroom with colleagues
  who are just going to make you feel worse by complaining
  about their lives, the boss, or the new impossible-to-meet
  budget goals. Seek out friends who inspire you.

- *Carve out some time to help others.* Volunteer your time and
  talents at a soup kitchen, hospital, or shelter for the home-
  less. The stresses people in these situations face will help
  you put yours in proportion.

- *Focus on positive things at mealtime.* The brain creates chemi-
  cals that counteract effective digestion when you worry, fret,
  argue, or process negative thoughts.

- *Improve your working environment.* If you have a desk job,
  make sure your chair is the right height and your work materials and equipment are where you won't strain your back
  or eyes.

- *Keep a calendar of emotions for a month or two.* See if you
  can pinpoint when you're dealing with PMS. When you're
  experiencing PMS, get plenty of rest, don't eat sweets, exercise as much as possible, and cut back on caffeine.

- *Spend some time each day outdoors.* Breathe some fresh air
  and feel the sunshine. Exercise outdoors, eat lunch outdoors,
  take weekend trips outdoors, sit by a sunny window, read a
  book on your porch, even if it's only for ten to fifteen minutes at a time.

- *Declare a decluttering campaign.* Clutter causes stress. Give yourself a reasonable amount of time, one month, to say good-bye to junk. Clean out closets and drawers a little at a time. Clean off your desk and clean out your purse and your wallet. Purging your personal space of clutter and organizing what's left can be very uplifting.

- *Make a list of things you're grateful for.* Don't forget the things we tend to take for granted—two eyes, two hands, two feet, and a brain.
- *Make a list of things that make you happy.* One woman who started such a list turned it into a whole book.
- *Consider that you may be feeling sorry for yourself and allowing negative circumstances to control you.* I was inspired by a woman who was a guest on a talk show. Although she was paralyzed from the waist down and destined to spend the rest of her life in a wheelchair, she didn't let this keep her down emotionally. She began a special exercise program for handicapped people.
- *Look your best for yourself.* Getting into the rut of being sloppy in your appearance can drag you down and add to your stress. If I find myself sinking into a negative mood, I take a fragrant bubble bath, wash and style my hair, and put on a pretty outfit. It makes me feel better when I like what I see in the mirror.
- *Start working on a project or putter at a hobby you enjoy.* Work is very healing.
- *Find a special place that refreshes and inspires you,* whether it's a park bench, a mountain trail, the beach, or the woods. Use it as a regular retreat in which to read or reflect.
- *Schedule a quiet time every day and say no to interruptions.* Most women unconsciously and automatically put the needs of others—spouse, kids, friends—before their own. Our sleep, phone calls, meals, even bathroom time are all fair

game. Establish a set quiet time each day—for example, between 2:30 and 3:00 P.M.—during which no one can ask for
anything, barring an emergency. If you retreat to the bathroom to soak in the tub, put a Do Not Disturb sign on the
door. Young children who don't take naps can be taught that
even if they don't go to sleep, they must have quiet time in
their own rooms looking at books, listening to tapes quietly,
or playing with quiet toys.

- *Stop doing everything yourself.* Learn to delegate. Sure, it
  may seem easier to put away the laundry yourself—just the
  way you like to see it in the drawers and linen closet—but in
  the long run it's better for you and your family members to
  share household chores. Clearly explain how to accomplish
  each chore, decide who will be responsible, then let go. So
  what if the carpet isn't vacuumed in perfect stripes. Does it
  really matter? Rethink your standards, if necessary. Cut yourself and your family members some slack.

- *Go on a short vacation by yourself.* Even if you've taken a
  family vacation recently, you need a vacation from your job as
  family manager.

- *Establish effective transition behaviors between your various
  roles and responsibilities.* It usually takes fifteen to twenty
  minutes to make the transition from a stressful day of business to relaxation or refreshing recreation. At our house we
  call this reentry time. Here are a few ideas:

  —Listen to soothing music or inspirational audiotapes on the
    drive home from work.

  —Take a catnap.

  —Take off your work uniform.

  —Put on a play uniform (tennis clothes, sweat suit, beach
    clothes).

  —Engage in a short exercise routine.

-Spend twenty minutes in prayer, meditation, or inspirational reading.

-Have a chat with a friend you enjoy.

-Walk your pet.

-Work in your garden.

-Play a musical instrument.

-Read a novel.

-Peruse a favorite magazine or catalog.

-Resolve not to discuss work with your spouse for one hour after you get home.

- *Plan ahead for times of extra stress,* such as the holiday season or before a big project at work.

-Sleep a little extra ahead of time.

-Cut back on the activities you can.

-Make sure you do your morning quiet time/meditation faithfully.

-Plan your time as efficiently as possible.

-Restrict the demands others impose on you.

-Don't add anything unnecessary to your schedule. Wait until the crunch is over to get your teeth cleaned.

- *Stick to your priorities.* Be firm with those who might clutter up your life with their priorities. Don't feel guilty about not doing what everyone wants you to do.

- *Make big life changes wisely.* It's easy to get stressed worrying about making good decisions. There's no foolproof method to make decisions that I know of, but these steps will help you have confidence that you're seeking to be as wise as possible.

-List your options. Just brainstorm and let the ink flow. Don't edit at this point.

-Think about your choices. Sort out your feelings about the options you wrote.

–Relate your choices to your priorities. What's really most important to you?

–Think about how your choices will affect the other members of your family.

–Make a decision and stick with it.

–Help yourself in every way possible to stick to your decision by telling someone the decision you've made, thus becoming accountable to that person. Be realistic about when you can make the change or start your new habit or action.

–Launch your new practice as strongly and vigorously as possible. Make it a big deal.

–Avoid too many changes at once. Whenever you can, plan major life changes—houses, jobs, adding to the people who live at your house—so they do not all occur at the same time.

* *Don't be a slave to the telephone.* Discipline yourself to use an answering machine or voice mail. Don't pick up the phone just because it rings. Talk to people when it's convenient for you.

* *Expect the unexpected.* Life is full of surprises, and children are predictably unpredictable. Remember that almost everything in life takes longer than anticipated. Plan accordingly so you have some breathing room.

* *Cut back on activities.* Learn to say no. Delete activities and commitments that are not fulfilling. Don't let other people "guilt" you into saying yes to things that aren't high on your list of priorities.

* *Learn to relax.* Consciously relax your brow. Drop your lower jaw. Avoid clenching your fists or holding on tight to objects; consciously relax your hands, especially when holding a pen, driving a car, or watching TV. Relax your stomach muscles. Breathe deeply.

* *Count your blessings.* Make a list of the little blessings in your life from just last week. If none come to mind, ask your-

self some questions: Has your car been running smoothly? Do you have hot water for a shower? Has someone told you that he or she cares? Do you have clothes to wear? Has a coworker complimented you? Is your roof not leaking? If it is, is it leaking in only three spots? Have you been able to make progress on a project? Has your child come home with a good grade?

- *Turn off the television.* As an average adult, you will gain more than thirty hours a week this way. Watch your intake of current events. The evening news is one of the goriest, most shocking programs on television.

- *Plan for free time.* Block it out on your calendar just as you would an important appointment.

- *Start an informal support group.* I've seen the wisdom of a support network played out in nature. When I was in northern California a few years ago, I took some time to walk around among the giant sequoia trees. Almost two thousand years old, these trees are more than two hundred feet high and seventy feet in circumference.

  I was surprised to learn that trees this big don't have massive, deep roots to help them withstand years of wind, rain, and erosion. They have shallow root systems, just below the ground. They grow in groves, their roots intertwining, so when the strong winds blow, they stabilize each other. Call it a support group. We humans need the same kind of help. We need to seek out like women and agree to be there for each other when the wind blows.

- *Create a morning ritual.* Begin each day with something that inspires or energizes you, like reading over a cup of hot coffee, journaling, exercising, or listening to music. For years I've had a morning ritual of getting up early and going to the Y to work out. I listen to inspirational music on the way there and back. When I come home I read a portion of the Bible and pray for my family and friends and for the coming events of the day.

• *Exercise.* When we exercise, our bodies produce endorphins, a naturally produced morphinelike substance that can deliver a feeling of peacefulness. These are the body's natural pain-killers. Exercise also serves as an outlet for pent-up stress caused by frustrations and troublesome thoughts.

• *Eat a healthful diet.* A nutritious, well-balanced diet is especially important when you are under stress because stress increases your metabolism, which raises your energy needs. Avoid a lot of caffeine.

• *Laugh.* Research has shown that laughter also triggers a release of endorphins. It's hard to think worrisome thoughts in the midst of a good laugh.

• *Seek out friends who inspire you and/or make you laugh.*

• *Give someone else a mental and emotional lift.* Showing appreciation and praising someone else is a good way to lift our own spirits.

• *Get plenty of sleep.* Fatigue can reduce your ability to deal with stress. But don't oversleep, as this can make you feel worse rather than better. Paradoxically, extra sleep often causes tiredness and headaches.

• *Take a vacation.* Take it from one who learned the hard way that a vacation can be just as stressful as the stress you left back home. Here are some tips for how to take a *relaxing, refreshing* vacation.

–Have realistic expectations. A vacation won't change your life in a week, but it can and will be refreshing if you let it be.

–Evaluate past vacations. Without raking yourself or anyone else over the coals, think of what could be improved.

—Give yourself permission to relax. Don't fall prey to free-floating guilt, which would have you working or doing something more useful.

—Laugh at obstacles and mishaps. Don't let things like long lines and flat tires flatten your fun.

—Decide on a vacation eating plan. Without forethought, overeating can ruin a vacation. Resistance is usually a little lower during vacations. Fatigue, frustration, and even boredom can stimulate indulgence.

> "If I had my life to live over again, I'd try to make more mistakes next time. I would relax. I'd be sillier than I have been on this trip. I would climb more mountains, swim more rivers, and watch more sunsets. I would have more actual troubles and less imaginary ones. Oh, I've had my moments, and if I had to do it again, I'd have more of them. In fact, I'd try to have nothing else, just moments, one after another. I would pick more daisies."
>
> —Nadine Stair (at age 89)

—Get regular exercise on your trip. Aim for a good balance between rest and activity.

- *Take a vacation from something.* If you can't take a vacation *to* someplace, taking a vacation *from* something can be restoring, even if it's only for twenty-four hours. For example, at home or in your office, decide that you're going to take a vacation from complaining or making any negative comments for twenty-four hours. A vacation from television and radio can help clear our minds. A vacation from the phone also helps.

The Bottom Line

- Stress is not a bad, frustrating circumstance in our lives. It is a normal psychophysiological process—our body and emotions working together—without which we would die.
- Stress is the reaction we have when small irritations, big catastrophes, or something really wonderful happens in our lives.
- We all have stressors in our lives we don't realize exist. Things such as poor lighting, an uncomfortable chair, and clutter can cause stress. We need to pay attention to all the factors affecting our emotions and stress level, including how much we're sleeping and exercising and what we're eating.
- We can control the way stress affects our lives by the way we choose to react. It's important to learn to see situations for what they are, not for what we imagine them to be. It's easy to blow things all out of proportion, needlessly raising our stress level.
- We need to take responsibility to change the things in our life that we *can* change, such as getting more sleep, eating wisely, and exercising.
- Cultivate a healthy social support system of family and friends.

NINE

The Spiritual Dimension
of You

"I do not think that I will ever reach a stage when I will say,
'This is what I believe. Finished.' What I believe is alive . . .
and open to growth."   —Madeleine L'Engle

Congratulations! If you've made it through the book to this
point, you're already learning new ways to care for yourself. You've covered a lot of information and read a lot of
tips on how to take control of your life and move in the direction of becoming your best self. The ideas you've read have been
about you—your dreams, your time, your body, your mind, your
emotions.

But as much as I believe in what I've written, I would be doing
you a disservice if I did not tell you that this information could
cause you more pain than satisfaction. The distance between a
woman who is committed to taking care of herself and being her
personal best and a woman who is self-absorbed and narcissistic is
a short one. If you begin to think that you are the center of the
universe and that everyone else should fall into orbit around your
plan for self-care and self-fulfillment, you may self-destruct. If taking care of yourself becomes your highest priority, I can virtually
guarantee that you will never experience the true happiness and
personal success you long for.

> Think of all the selfish people you know who are happy. (Short list, huh?) Now think of all the generous people you know who are happy. Which would you rather be?
>
> "A woman wrapped up in herself makes a small package."　　—Unknown

Who's at the Center of Your Universe?

Our definition of personal success is an extension of the satisfaction of our soul. We are all, I believe, created with a spiritual hunger. Instinctively we know that we need more than the externals of life can provide, as nice as they are. This longing within us evidences itself in timeless questions:

We want to know where we came from and where our best efforts might take us.

We wonder if there is a world beyond what we can see—and if there is a Creator who crafted and cares for us and can give us the inner strength to meet the challenges of life.

We want to know how we can live at peace with ourselves and those around us, and what will happen to us when we die.

We want assurance that what we do matters somehow, that it makes a difference.

Some people get fidgety when you start talking about spiritual issues. Believe me, I understand. There are religious people who make me want to run the other way. I've found, though, that spirituality has less to do with external things—rules, regulations, cathedrals, and rituals—than it does with internal convictions, aspirations, and attitudes—what matters to

> "Our souls are hungry for meaning, for the sense that we have figured out how to live so that our lives matter, so that the world will be at least a little bit different for our having passed through it."
>
> —Harold Kushner

me on a soul-deep, life-and-death level. These include things such as how I view the universe, how I deal with guilt and forgiveness, where I get my standard of what's right and wrong, how I treat others, how I see myself in relation to other people, what's most important to me—the people I love, the tasks I give my energy to, the sensibility I want my life to exude, the ways I use the talents I've been given. The decisions I make and actions I take regarding these all-important issues both reveal and spring from who dwells at the center of my universe. Everybody exercises faith; the question is, in what?

Where do you find meaning?
What is really important to you?
What is your source of peace?
How is it working?

In my late teenage years I had to learn the hard way that I wasn't doing a very good job of running my life, much less the universe. I reached a point when I didn't want to continue life as it was. Some friends whom I admired encouraged me to investigate the claims of God in the Old and New Testaments. Because of the peace and joy in their lives that I observed and wanted for myself, I accepted their challenge. I found that even my best secondhand opinions about God were in no way worthy of the loving God I found on the pages of my Bible. He gave my life a whole new meaning, and it has never been the same. I began a lifelong journey with God. There are potholes and obstacles in my path, to be sure. But I don't experience them alone. God is with me every step of the way.

I know that not everyone has the same spiritual beliefs

> "The most important thing about a man is his view of the universe." —G. K. Chesterton

that I do. I can only share with you the difference my faith has made in my life. Spiritual issues are personal but vital. They define your values, highlight your aspirations, and ultimately affect everything you do. They affect the changes you want to make in your life and how you define personal success. They provide the inner motivation not only to value and take care of yourself but to be your best for a purpose and calling far beyond your self-interest.

Not Just a Part, but the Whole

In one way, it's harder for me to talk about the spiritual part of myself than it is to talk about any of the other categories. Not because I'm reluctant to talk about my relationship with God—I'm not. It's hard because my spiritual life is not separate from all other parts of my life. In a way, God is neither apart from my everyday life nor just a part of it. He is in all of it, from the time I get up in the morning through every transaction or interaction I have—with everybody from Bill and the boys to the people I work with to the mail carrier and the clerk at the supermarket.

Lest you think I'm randomly inserting my spiritual views into this book, I must tell you that the principles, strategies, and tips I've learned about living a well-managed, satisfying life—from taking care of my body to dealing with anger in healthy ways to running my home smoothly to balancing competing demands for my time and attention—have come from years of studying

> STOP: Slow down so you can observe.
> LOOK: Observe the world around you; look for the wonders and miracles.
> LISTEN: Pay attention to others, to nature, to your heart. What is God saying?

and applying principles from the Bible to everyday life. I continue to be surprised at its freshness and relevance to my life.

I wish we could just sit down and have a cup of coffee. If we had the chance to spend some time together, I would share with you my own spiritual quest. How a desire for peace, satisfaction, and meaning in my life led me to examine whether the Bible was just a book of stories with nice morals or a book of truth about the universe, men and women, and their Creator. I would tell you that through my failures, successes, questions, doubts, and subsequent search I found the peace, satisfaction, and meaning I was looking for. I would describe how my faith affects my attitudes and actions on a daily basis, and gives me the ability to face the future with courage and confidence.

If you could follow me through the day, you would see that the principles in the Bible help me maintain priorities and keep my balance. You would see that God is not peripheral, but the person at the center of my universe and the center of my life. He is the one who gives me the ability to be the best wife, mother, friend, and professional I can be. As important as my work is, as worthy a project as becoming my personal best is, I need something beyond myself at the center of my universe. I need someone beyond myself to call me to a personal best I could never imagine on my own—a best that stretches beyond my selfish agendas and reaches out to the world in ways more satisfying than I could dream of.

No Done Deals

> "There is an internal landscape, a geography of the soul; we search for its outlines all our lives." —Josephine Hart

Please don't get me wrong: I am not saying that I have "arrived" spiritually. Sometimes I can be exercising and eating well, reading a stimulating book and working on a new project—

everything going great—and get so wrapped up in myself and my work, I begin to lose balance and perspective. My mood takes a turn for the worse, and I find myself looking at a woman in the mirror held captive by her own selfishness. Other times nothing seems to be going right; I spend my days juggling crises. At times like these, I dream of having a genie I could command to solve my problems rather than a God who wants to use my problems to grow me into a stronger person. Then there are the days when I fail for the hundredth time to break a bad habit or be more patient and loving toward my family, and I feel like a total failure. And every once in a while I have really bad days when all I have are thoughts of despair: "I just can't go on . . . I will never change . . . I can't cope." I know then that it's time to go back to the basics of what I believe about God and what he is making of me.

As with our body and mind, our spiritual development is never a done deal. There are endless possibilities and untapped potential to be revealed in all of us. Life is a spiritual journey, the most important you and I can embark on.

One of the authors who has greatly influenced my spiritual thinking is George MacDonald, a nineteenth-century Scottish colleague of Charles Dickens, Robert Louis Stevenson, and Lewis Carroll. From MacDonald's writings I learned that the essence of spirituality is not how much a person knows, but how willing one is to learn; not where a person stands, but in which direction he is progressing; not what doubts he harbors, but into what truth such doubts eventually lead; not how spiritual one may appear in the eyes of other people, but how much truth one is seeking in the quietness of one's own heart.

> "Where there are no doubts, no questions, no perplexities, there can be no growth. . . . Doubts are the only means through which we can enlarge our spiritual selves."
>
> —George MacDonald

I'm not saying my faith is better than yours. I simply encourage you to ask yourself honestly if what you believe adequately covers the serious issues of life:

- Does your faith give your life meaning, purpose, and peace?
- Does your faith support you in every phase of your life: adolescence, young adulthood, middle age, old age? Does it support you during marriage crises, financial crises, children's crises, energy crises, cultural crises, and moral crises?
- Does it deal with guilt and forgiveness?
- Does it answer the question of evil and still give you hope?
- Does it provide a way for you to look realistically at the problems of life without despair?

Is Your Faith Adequate for Tough Times?

Let me explain why this chapter is important. None of us has a perfect life. This is not a perfect world. We all deal with sickness, pain, loneliness, disappointment, insecurity, failure, and death. How we face the trouble in our lives, and how it affects us for the rest of our lives, depends on our faith. George MacDonald said it like this:

Sometimes a thunderbolt will shoot from a clear sky; sometimes into the life of a peaceful individual, without any warning of a gathered storm, something terrible will fall. And from that moment on everything is changed. That life is no more what it was. Better it ought to be, worse it may be. The result depends on the life itself and its response to the invading storm of trouble. Forever after its spiritual weather is altered. But for the one who believes in God, such rending and frightful catastrophes never come but where they are turned around for good in his own life and in others he touches.

Are You Better or Bitter?

One of the things I have discovered is that God is not going to shelter me from the pain of life, but he will go through the pain with me, making it possible for me to become better, not bitter, for these experiences.

Is your God able to carry you through the bad times as well as the good? I encourage you to schedule some time in the very near future when you won't be interrupted, and to use this time to think about spiritual issues and their relevance in your life. And please, don't make a decision about God based just on what you hear or see in other people or what you read in the newspaper.

Think of it this way: pretend you had never heard of Mozart and were asked to decide whether he was a gifted composer. You had to make your decision about Mozart by listening to me play his Piano Concerto No. 20 in D minor. Trust me, you wouldn't have a full appreciation of his genius. But if you listened to an accomplished musician who had studied and practiced the works of Mozart, you would get a better picture. Imagine you were somehow able to hear him play in person; you would be able to experience him for who he truly is. In my mind, it's the same when it comes to forming an opinion about God. Go to the Bible and let God speak for himself. Be honest about your questions and doubts as you search for answers. If the Bible is truly God's word to mankind, then it will speak to you in profound ways if you are honestly trying to listen.

"I want to know God's
thoughts."   —Albert Einstein

Decide What You Believe and Let Those Beliefs Guide Your Life

Beliefs not lived out are really not beliefs at all. Our beliefs involve what we do more than what we think or say. That's a big part of our lifelong spiritual journey: learning to live out what we believe.

To help me in my quest to do just that, I set aside some time a number of years ago to write down the spiritual principles I wanted to influence my attitudes and actions. I wrote sixty or so of these in a journal and since then have kept a laminated copy of these principles in the front of my calendar notebook. This way I can easily read them before a meeting, on an airplane, in a doctor's office, or at any time to remind me of the woman I want to be and the values I want to live by. I list a few of the principles here to show you what I mean. I encourage you to write out your own and keep them easily accessible.

My Beliefs and Aspirations

- Every day is a gift. Each moment of life is a sacred privilege. Therefore, there is no unimportant time.
- God is always nearer to me than anything else.
- I should care for everything, because everything belongs to God.
- The best thing I can pass on to my children is a heritage of righteousness, truth, love for God, and service to mankind. This is a more lasting inheritance than any earthly fortune.
- How I face difficulties shows who I really am.
- God sees the whole parade, when I can see only one float at a time.
- There are 350 passages in the Bible that tell me to "fear not."
- Sometimes God answers my prayers by giving me what I ask

for. Other times he answers by helping me get along without
what I ask for. Many times, what I ask for I don't need at all.
God knows what is best for me.

- A strong indication of my spiritual maturity is my ability to
demonstrate the love of Christ to those who mistreat me.

- When my life is filled with adversity and my human strength
is drained, Christ's invitation becomes more and more attractive. "Come unto me, all that labor and are heavy laden, and
I will give you rest" (Matthew 11:28).

- I will strive not to get so busy with my plans, goals, and projects that God must speak to me from Jeremiah 35:14: "I
have spoken unto you, rising early and speaking; but ye hear-
kened not unto me."

- The business of my life is not to get as much as I can, but to
do justly, love mercy, and walk humbly with my God.

- May I never forget that people are more important than projects and prosperity.

- In order to lead others in a worthy manner, I must listen for
God's direction in my own life.

Moving On in Your Spiritual Journey

Where are you on your spiritual journey? Wherever you are, taking time to ask hard questions and search for answers is important.
Here are some ways to develop your spiritual life.

- When you face a dilemma, say to God, "Please give me guidance and help." After you ask, be quiet and listen with your
heart and mind. He promised: "Call to me and I will answer
you and tell you great and unsearchable things you do not
know" (Jeremiah 33:3).

- Read a portion of the Bible every day.

- Read other inspirational books. Some of my favorites are *The Return of the Prodigal* by Henri Nouwen, *My Utmost for His Highest* by Oswald Chambers, and *A Shepherd Looks at Psalm 23* by Phillip Keller.
- When you read a book by an author who speaks to you, try to read more of his or her writings. Some of the authors who have nourished my spirit are C. S. Lewis, Francis Schaeffer, Os Guiness, Max Lucado, and Charles Swindoll.
- Spend time with spiritual people you admire. Learn from them.
- Jot down ideas, prayers, verses, and quotes from books that give you insight and wisdom.
- If you wonder, "How do I know that there is a God?" perhaps a more pertinent question would be: "If there is in fact a God, how can I find him?"
- Practice Sabbath rest. Someone once said, "God rested—and he wasn't tired." Rest is an opportunity for contemplation, reflection, and recollection of what's at the center of the universe.
- Collect inspirational music; music is the language of the soul.
- Try to watch at least one sunrise or sunset each week.
- Remind yourself to be conscious of God's presence—in quiet moments at home, in sleepless moments in the middle of the night.
- Take a walk in the park with a small child, adopting his or her sense of wonder. See what the child sees and give yourself permission to express the same awe of nature.
- On your way home from work, pause to remark on the beauty of the sky or terrain.

> "I love to think of nature as an unlimited broadcasting station through which God speaks to us every hour, if we will only tune in."
> —George Washington Carver

> "To be alive, to be able to see, to walk, to have houses, music, paintings—it's all a miracle. I have adopted the technique of living life from miracle to miracle." —Arthur Rubinstein

- When you eat something today, really taste it—and be thankful for the taste buds that let you enjoy it.
- Note the different textures you brush up against today. Celebrate the diversity of life.

- In a difficult situation, look for at least one thing you can be grateful for. The old adage about silver linings is very often true.
- Write a thank-you note to someone who has had a positive impact on your life.
- Practice spontaneous gratitude. When something positive happens to you or someone you love, pause and thank God.
- Give thanks before meals.
- When you get into an ungrateful state of mind and begin to gripe and complain, try to see yourself in the future—how you want to have responded to the situation.
- Celebrate something good that happens to you by doing something good for someone else.
- Be mindful of your blessings every day.
- Keep a prayer journal. Write down your requests and record the answers. This will help you build your awareness of the spiritual.
- Make a list of the ways you've fallen short and want to feel forgiven. Turn what you write down into a prayer.

> "The best way to show my gratitude to God is to accept everything, even my problems, with joy." —Mother Teresa

- When you act in a way that is hurtful to yourself or others, ask forgiveness— from the other person or yourself and from God.
- Forgive others in your life

as you would like to be forgiven.

- Share spiritual ideas with a friend. We can deepen our spiritual life both by hearing others' beliefs and by saying our own out loud. (Or consider starting an informal growth group. Meet with several people once a month to discuss a book or topic.)

> "The longest journey is the journey inward."
> —Dag Hammarskjöld

- Worship regularly.
- Take time to reflect on important spiritual ideas—the ones you want your life to emulate. As you turn them over in your mind, you'll find yourself living out the principles that have become a part of you.
- Take the time to get to know an older woman whose spirituality you respect.

Love Your Neighbor as Yourself: A Dozen Everyday Acts of Spirituality

- Practice self-control—let your husband wear his ratty sweatshirt in peace.
- Tell your son or daughter: "If I could choose any kid in the world, I'd choose you!"
- Listen to family members with your eyes as well as with your ears.
- Hug your moody teenager.
- If you tell your husband you'll bury the hatchet, don't leave the handle sticking out.

> "The ordinary acts we practice every day at home are of more importance to the soul than their simplicity might suggest."
> —Thomas Moore

- Offer practical help to someone who crosses your path today.
- If you offend your spouse or child, say you're sorry—sincerely.
- Plan extra spots at your family's holiday table and fill them with people who would otherwise be left alone.
- Load the dishwasher even when it's not your turn.
- Call your mother-in-law. Tell her how much you appreciate your husband.
- Say something encouraging to someone at least once a day.
- Do something every day to make the world a better place.

The Bottom Line

- Faith is not using religious-sounding words in the daytime. It is asking your deepest questions at night—and then getting up and living out your day, being alert for answers.
- If you're feeling at the end of your rope, do some soul-searching. Don't be afraid to ask hard questions about life.
- All of us must decide who's running the universe—and who's going to run our life.
- Our relationship with God takes time and persistence, just like any other relationship.
- We never "arrive." Our spiritual development is never a done deal.
- Practice being thankful for what you have, and you'll find there's a lot to be thankful about. Practice asking for guidance—and you're likely to get it.

TEN

What Personal Success Means to You

ONE of the strong desires of my heart is to encourage women (including myself) to discover and tap into their incredible potential and experience personal success in life. Because we are each unique, this means many different things to each one of us.

I don't know the desires of your heart or what you struggle with in life. I don't know your age, race, or educational background. But I do know that there are fundamental principles of life that apply across the board, no matter what our circumstances.

For thirty years I've collected information from many different sources—books, people, experiences—about how to be a successful wife, mother, friend, and professional. I've learned a lot over the years, but I've still got a long way to go. Listed on the following pages are some life principles about personal success that I've learned from other people or from my own experiences. I encourage you to write your name in the blank provided and as you read through the list, mark the ones that speak to you. Personalize those principles by stating them aloud. For example, say, "I, Rebecca, understand that my inner attitude determines the outer aspects of my life." Then envision yourself living the life described in each principle that you marked.

Come back to this chapter on days when you're not living the life you want to live or being the woman you want to be and go through the exercise again. We all fail sometimes and disappoint ourselves. When this happens, remember to cut yourself some slack and let your setbacks serve as stepping-stones to a better path. From experience, I know if you do this you'll find yourself making progress toward becoming the woman you aspire to be.

I, _____, . . .

- know my inner attitude determines the outer aspects of my life.
- am substituting new positive habits for old negative ones.
- understand that first I make my decisions, then my decisions make me.
- believe that with God all things are possible.
- believe the best of myself and others.
- spread joy to others.
- am a good manager of my time.
- influence others in positive ways.
- have been given the precious gift of life with limitless possibilities.
- invest my time in worthwhile efforts.
- take time to think, for my ideas make up who I am.
- am growing better as I'm growing older.
- am living my own biography. I can be heroine or villain, great or mediocre.
- believe that worship, wherever it is experienced, is an inner adventure.
- hold my tongue because I know if I lose my temper, I lose.
- take time to live as well as make a living.
- encourage and appreciate others.

- fill my moments with enriching experiences that give new meaning and depth to my life.
- am making the world a better place to be.
- have fourteen hundred and forty minutes each day to choose how I'm going to live.
- find time to love and enjoy my family.
- find time to enjoy my friends.
- am committed to a regular exercise program.
- don't always look for the closest parking place at the mall.
- let myself cry sometimes.
- am becoming the woman I aspire to be.
- practice the presence of God.
- am a woman of excellence.
- believe that no failure is final, unless I don't get up.
- know there's more to life than increasing its speed.
- rise above petty irritations.
- am self-disciplined.
- strive to change what can be changed.
- adapt myself to what cannot be changed.
- am fun to be around.
- give thanks daily.
- take the high road.
- am setting a good example for my children.
- bring out the best in others.
- enjoy my own company.
- get away alone on a regular basis to think and pray.
- do not allow negative people to determine my mood.
- nurture my children's unique gifts and talents.
- look my best for myself.
- am learning to express my emotions in healthful ways.
- believe the greatest use of life is to spend it on something that will outlast it.

- seek to follow God's will.
- enjoy the beauty of good music.
- am loving and kindhearted.
- volunteer my time and resources to help others.
- see my cup as half full instead of half empty.
- am never bored.
- am committed to being the best I can be.
- give myself the freedom to do things I've always wanted to do.
- schedule regular times to play.
- like who I see looking back at me in the mirror.
- am a valuable person.
- have incredible potential.
- am generous.
- expect to be successful.
- am committed to being a lifelong learner.
- can be counted on.
- am not ordinary.
- limit my TV time.
- am prepared.
- am always improving my vocabulary.
- wisely manage money.
- fill my mind with quality reading material.
- believe that God works all things together for good.
- discipline myself today so I'll be my best tomorrow.
- set personal goals.
- celebrate the successes of others.
- surround myself with good books.
- am a loving wife.
- am a good friend.
- know how to say "I'm sorry."
- have friends who push me to be my best.

- am a person of my word.
- am not afraid of change.
- start the day on a positive note.
- have my own style.
- am friendly.
- get along well with most people.
- am a leader.
- try to learn something from everyone.
- help others see their value.
- congratulate myself at the end of the day for what I've accomplished.
- work hard when I work and play hard when I play.
- make use of small bits of time.
- believe that pain is inevitable, but misery is optional.
- am not a procrastinator.
- am learning to make good decisions.
- carry on meaningful traditions.
- ask myself regularly, "Is this the best possible use of my time?"
- am a self-starter.
- can laugh at myself.
- have good posture.
- pray regularly.
- am not afraid of the future.
- say no to requests and jobs that do not fit into my priorities and goals.
- am not afraid to ask for help.
- am flexible.
- eat wisely.
- am a person of integrity.
- am generous with my possessions.
- am a hard worker.
- take risks.

- do not overeat.
- live a balanced life.
- am a good neighbor.
- spend some quiet time daily listening to God with my heart.
- am patient with myself and others.
- have an attitude of gratitude.
- am creating a warm and welcoming home.
- am considerate of the feelings of others.
- dream grand dreams.
- deliver more than I promise.
- am a good family manager.
- have good health habits.
- am influencing our culture for good.
- take care of my skin.
- keep a journal of my thoughts and prayers.
- read good books.
- write thank-you notes promptly.
- am not sloppy.
- am helpful.
- am not afraid to stand up for what I believe is right.
- help others succeed.
- have a lot of common sense.
- don't dwell on my mistakes.
- spend money wisely.
- do not gossip or speak critically of others in public.
- am growing in my faith.
- know what my priorities are and try to live by them.
- express anger in healthy ways.
- stay away from high-fat foods.
- honestly try to see things from the other person's point of view.
- do not need to take the credit.

- am tenacious.
- do not always have to be right.
- can be trusted.
- am not cynical.
- turn problems into opportunities.
- am gracious and forgiving.
- am continuously improving.
- think before I talk.
- bring out the best in people.
- am living more wisely and feeling less stressed.
- am learning to be more organized.
- learn new skills regularly.
- put others at ease.
- take vacations.
- do not let others determine my self-worth.
- learn from my failures.
- constantly expand my knowledge.
- keep up with my extended family.
- delegate wisely.
- am a good listener.
- don't expect perfection from others.
- have good manners.
- drink six to eight glasses of water each day.
- take genuine interest in other people.
- am not a complainer.
- have a good sense of humor.
- am a creative problem solver.
- am resourceful.
- look for mentors to learn from.
- arrive on time at appointments.
- am a good conversationalist.
- have a morning ritual that helps me start the day off right.

- have hobbies I enjoy.
- smile a lot.
- am thankful for the privilege of voting, and do so at election time.
- do not let myself engage in self-pity.
- do not spend more money than I make.
- get plenty of sleep.
- am committed to doing the right thing.
- take care of my belongings.
- have a good social support system.
- live by the Golden Rule.
- schedule ways to have fun as a family each week.
- take vitamins.
- learn a new fact each day.
- strength-train at least three times each week.
- practice regular hospitality.
- am simplifying my life.
- tell the truth.
- do not let limitations hold me back.
- care for the natural resources of the earth.
- see problems as opportunities for growth.
- avoid impulse buying.
- first look for the two-by-four in my own eye, if I see a splinter in someone else's eye.
- believe that people are more important than projects.
- obey the law.
- evaluate myself regularly and envision who I want to be.
- have a lot of good ideas.
- do not have to be first in line.
- strive to live what I say I believe.
- influence people for good.
- am a patient driver.

- remember people's names.
- don't preach when someone close to me fails.
- respect older people.
- encourage others to be their best.
- do not seek to get revenge when someone hurts me.
- thank those who help me.
- keep secrets secret.
- am growing in my knowledge of God.
- know how to receive graciously, as well as give.
- go out of my way to help others.
- forget old hurts.
- take time to talk to children.
- laugh at other people's jokes.
- am better today than I was last week.
- feel good about who I am becoming.

"Your life becomes what you think."   —Marcus Aurelius

PARTING WORDS

What has this book prompted you to do? Who are you becoming and what are your dreams? What's working for you that might help other women be personally successful? Please write or e-mail us your comments to the addresses below. Visit us on the Web at www.familymanager.com for seminar dates and other helpful books and products. Or call or write to:

Kathy Peel
Family Manager, Inc.
P.O. Box 50577
Nashville, Tennessee 37205
615-376-5619
e-mail: familymanager@familymanager.com
Web site: www.familymanager.com

And remember . . .

"In the long run, we hit only what we aim high at. Aim high."
                                        —Henry David Thoreau

Index

ABOUT THE AUTHOR

Kathy Peel is the bestselling author of fifteen books. She is founder and president of Family Manager, Inc., a company committed to providing excellent resources and products to help families make their home a good place to be.

She is editor in chief of www.familymanager.com and writes regularly for *Family Circle*, *Sesame Street Parents*, and clubmom.com. She speaks frequently at conferences and conventions and is a popular guest on television and radio programs, including frequent appearances on *The Oprah Winfrey Show*.